What Peo

No Pa

CW01498464

An inspiring story of vision and deep love and connection with the land. Katie and Luke's inspirational passion for Wild Finca is felt on every page of this book. The journey is not an easy one, yet you are left feeling that the landscape is in good hands, and you cannot help but share the vision that one day, Wild Finca will be filled with the buzz of insects, the songs of long-lost bird species and even, possibly, the howl of the wolf. A wonderful read that restores a faith that landscapes such as these can, once again, see nature flourish in all its wild glory.
WildlifeKate, wildlife enthusiast and educator

A beautifully woven story that takes your hand through the mountains of Asturias and makes you feel as connected to it as the lawn in your backyard. As Katie and Luke's story develops and grows, just like their family and farm, so deepens your connection and willingness for their finca to flourish. As Katie invites us into her home and walks us across her pasture and meadows, we become enriched by tales of rewilding. Katie charms through her writing as she recounts the highs and lows of management, motherhood and as a custodian of this special conservation-led environment. This story left me inspired, my horizons feeling broader than ever before, the flame of hope for our neighbours on this planet ablaze and awakened, with all credit to the incomprehensible hard work and dedication of Luke and Katie, and beautifully surmised in *No Paradise with Wolves*.
Elle Kaye, conservationist and taxidermist

This immersive and inspirational book invites the reader to fall in love with nature again and you can't help but oblige. No matter where in the world you are, you find yourself side by side with Katie and Luke, as they make their way to becoming the custodians of a beautiful Spanish finca, nestled amongst the mountains of Asturias. Katie doesn't shy away from the trials and tribulations of prioritising biodiversity in a traditional farming landscape, yet their successes punctuate every chapter in the form of the returning flora and fauna. The content of this story is as beautifully diverse as the land they are so lovingly tending. A thoroughly enjoyable read, with comedic anecdotes and relatable tales of family life, the story of Wild Finca has filled my head with ideas and heart with hope. Not only is *No Paradise with Wolves* a book about restoring nature, Katie's honest account of raising their children in a wild environment sews the seed for other parents, like me, to join them in raising the custodians of the future.

Gemma Shooter, rewilding communicator, illustrator, and animal behaviourist

Can humans play a beneficial role within a habitat? Luke, Katie, and their young family are shining examples of just this. By telling their story, they share a hope that will warm hearts and inspire minds.

Rebecca Hosking, pioneer of agriwilding and founder of the Forever Flock

No Paradise with Wolves

A Journey of Rewilding and Resilience

No Paradise with Wolves

A Journey of Rewilding and Resilience

By Katie Stacey

EARTH
BOOKS

London, UK
Washington, DC, USA

CollectiveInk

First published by Earth Books, 2025
Earth Books is an imprint of Collective Ink Ltd.,
Unit 11, Shepperton House, 89 Shepperton Road, London, N1 3DF
office@collectiveinkbooks.com
www.collectiveinkbooks.com
www.collectiveinkbooks.com/earth-books/

For distributor details and how to order please visit the 'Ordering' section on our website.

Text copyright: Katie Stacey 2024

ISBN: 978 1 80341 852 0
978 1 80341 970 1 (ebook)
Library of Congress Control Number: 2024947264

A CIP catalogue record for this book is available from the British Library.

Design: Lapiz Digital Services

UK: Printed and bound by CPI Group (UK) Ltd, Croydon, CR0 4YY
Printed in North America by CPI GPS partners

We operate a distinctive and ethical publishing philosophy in all areas of our business, from our global network of authors to production and worldwide distribution.

Contents

For my heart, Luke, Roan and Albus.
And for our home, Wild Finca.

Part 1

Sowing the Seed

Chapter 1

El Mexicano

I was sat outside, basking in the weak February sun at our new local bar. My parents, visiting for the first time since our move the previous month, were with me. We were waiting for Luke to return with another round of vermút (a syrup-like fortified wine), poured generously from the aged oak barrel set on the bar. Luke soon appeared with our drinks and, if he had understood correctly, an invitation to visit the finca (farm) of a local ganadero (farmer). Said ganadero appeared a few moments later, introducing himself as El Mexicano and graciously extending the invitation to all of us.

He was as round as he was short, with wisps of wild white hair on his head, and an immense bushy white beard. He followed up his offer with some vague pointing into the hills, but it was quite hard to understand him. He spoke the local Asturian dialect, quite different to the little Castilian Spanish we knew. Fortunately, Luke had a better grasp than I of the language, and, aided by the vermút, he managed to come to some sort of understanding with the ganadero. I thought I caught an offer of blue-egg laying chickens, which sounded mythical and most likely incorrect. And with that El Mexicano said his goodbyes to the rest of the regulars sat outside, climbed into a beat-up old white Peugeot, and drove off in the same direction he'd just gestured.

A few weeks after that first meeting we found ourselves following that same road El Mexicano had driven off on, in search of his farm. With a bit of direction along the way (everyone knew everyone in these parts), we finally found the old white Peugeot parked up by a steep rocky pathway. And, as the farmer next door directed us, we struck off along the treacherous looking animal route. After a five-minute climb we came to a fence and beyond that spotted a dilapidated old farmhouse, guarded by a fearsome looking mastín with a ferocious bark. Fortunately, El Mexicano appeared, called the dog off and invited us in. We passed under a cluster of trees where an impressive looking horse and cart stood waiting. Crossed a boggy pasture where the odd cow stood grazing. A smaller fenced off meadow held thirty plus goats, and we made our way towards the house where chickens and Muscovy Ducks scratched about. Up close it was now clear that the old farmhouse was derelict. Downstairs, in what used to be the kitchen, a broody hen sat on eggs in a long-abandoned oven. The rest of the space now used to store animal feed. The upstairs seemed to be used for the sole purpose of drying walnuts, something we ended up being gifted by the bag on subsequent visits. Beside the farmhouse a small stable housed a regular looking pig suckling five Wild Boar piglets. El Mexicano explained that he'd found them abandoned on his land after hunters had killed the sow.

Beneath the hórreo—a structure synonymous with Asturian fincas and traditionally used for grain storage—was an enclosure that served as the chicken and duck coop. In the main part of the hórreo, El Mexicano showed us the chicks, including two he wanted to gift us, which indeed laid blue eggs. But before we could receive our gifts, he put us to work: the goats and sheep needed feeding, the eggs needed collecting, and the cow needed milking. The cow had been patiently stood by the old farmhouse door since our arrival, and once all the pre-mentioned errands were completed, the gentle dairy cow was seen to. El Mexicano took a precarious seat on an ancient wooden three-legged milking stall and got to it, making the process look simple enough, but when I was offered the opportunity to try, I soon realised that it was not. I could not get any milk to come out, no matter how hard I squeezed. El Mexicano chuckled at my attempts, and he tried to show me, starting at the top and rolling all the way down. But I just couldn't get the hang of it, and there were still jobs to be done, so he'd resumed the task. He'd proceeded to fill three empty one-litre Coca-Cola bottles with fresh milk. One bottle was for El Mexicano, one for us and the final bottle was later poured over stale bread for the farm cats, who'd thus far spent their time trying to trip us up as we'd gone about our duties.

We asked why he was called El Mexicano? He explained that the name El Mexicano (translation The Mexican) had come from the fact that his family had been part of those who'd ventured to South America during the rule of the Spanish Empire. He himself had never left mainland Spain, apart from when he'd gone to the Canary Islands for his military training.

With the cow milked, the animals fed, and now laden with a box containing two white chickens, a Coca-Cola bottle of fresh milk and a wicker basket of Easter coloured eggs, we thought our visit was coming to an end. But El Mexicano, who seemed to enjoy the company, was not going to let us go so easily. He led us back the way we'd come, to the horse and cart, and introduced us to the giant horse, appropriately named Spartacus. Next El Mexicano requested Luke's help loading the cart with firewood, whilst I was left responsible of correctly placing Spartacus, so that the cart could be loaded. Having grown up with horses I initially felt confident handling the gentle giant. Accurately co-ordinating the cart behind him, however, did not come so easily.

When the cart was full of wood, chickens, eggs and milk, El Mexicano insisted we go to his house for a coffee. I was to ride on the cart with him, and Luke would follow in our car. But first we needed to negotiate the same treacherous rocky pathway we'd arrived by, and again, having made the mistake of letting El Mexicano know that I was comfortable with horses, I was left in charge of leading Spartacus and the now piled high cart. It was exhausting. El Mexicano and Luke followed behind, El

Mexicano talking Asturian at a million miles an hour and Luke trying his best to keep up with it all.

We did not follow the same path all the way down, to where we were parked, but instead took a right joining a more pronounced track that followed down through a small spinney to a little stream. Running water was a step too far for my newly acquired horse and cart skills, and so El Mexicano took charge, hopping spritely onto the cart. Standing astride the wood pile he expertly geed Spartacus forward, and the horse crossed the frothing waters like a pro, coming out the other side with cart contents all intact.

Back on the tarmac road El Mexicano pulled out a pair of bright red French knickers and attached them to either side of the trailer's license plate. I can only guess they were in lieu of safety reflectors. Once the horse and cart had been made road safe, El Mexicano helped me up onto the cart, motioning to a seat beside him amongst the firewood, and we hit the road, while Luke walked back by himself to collect the car. Throughout the journey El Mexicano would ask questions. I could tell they were questions by his intonation, but what exactly he was questioning I couldn't quite make out. So I nodded and made polite noises in reply when the time felt right. My Spanish language experience included the project in the South of Spain on the Iberian Lynx, and five months managing a ranch in Nicaragua. But on both occasions most of my interactions had been with English speakers, and so, despite my time spent living in Spanish speaking countries, my grasp of the language was embarrassingly poor. But El Mexicano didn't seem to mind, and he nattered away regardless of my lack of input.

Twenty minutes later we arrived at the village where El Mexicano lived. His home was a quaint little stone cottage. Five pairs of wellington boots, most mismatched and all in varying degrees of deterioration, lay on the front doorstep. More cats, and a pretty border collie, greeted us. El Mexicano busied himself unloading the cart and unhooking Spartacus. Once free he directed me to hose Spartacus down, while he neatly folded away the French knickers, and then he wheeled the cart underneath another hórreo. Spartacus was fed before being turned out in a field down the road, with a full hay net and a bucket of fresh water. Once the animals had all been seen to, next it was our turn. Fresh coffee with even fresher milk, and then El Mexicano set to work on fried potatoes, finished off with the eggs we collected just hours earlier, poached in the potato's frying oil. It was all delicious, and we've adopted that simple combination as our go-to comfort food to this day.

Chapter 2

Poop for the Veg Patch

We'd made the decision to re-locate to Spain after a successful five months spent in Andalucía, doing a project on what was then the rarest cat species in the world, the Iberian lynx. However, our search for a property to rent, and a place we truly connected with in the south, proved elusive. So, I'd given in to Luke's badgering to visit northern Spain, specifically Asturias.

For much of our Iberian Lynx project we had stayed in a beautiful little B&B called Villa Matilda. Owned by a Galician lady, who we'd become good friends with, and who'd warned us, when we'd mentioned an interest in Asturias, that it always rained there. To me, moving to somewhere that was as wet as the UK seemed a bit ridiculous. Yet Luke managed to persuade me that the wildlife would be worth it. Iberian Wolf, Cantabrian Brown Bear, Bearded Vulture, Golden Eagle and all manner of other exotic wildlife called the province home. Plus, rain was what made the area one of the Iberian Peninsula's green jewels. And so I agreed on a week's recce in November of 2017.

Amidst the exploring we'd been actively looking for somewhere to rent, but we kept hitting the same stumbling block. Unless we could match what the landlords made during the summer months, then they weren't interested in a long-term rental. From April through to September they made enough money that they could afford to leave their properties empty the rest of the year. And our budget was never going to match a summer's taking. Those that did consider us included a converted railway station at the foot of the entrance to Los Lagos, locally known as the gateway to the Picos. The one picture of the house online had been taken from the outside, and from this angle it looked quite sweet. It was next to a stream, and not too far out of a rather buzzy town. What the photo didn't show was that it sat right beside a huge religious sanctuary, that attracted thousands of pilgrims annually. And the pretty little stream meant the building itself suffered from terrible damp. Plus, the hunting themed interior (a deer and/or boar head graced every room) didn't give it the cosiest atmosphere. In fact, most of the houses we saw had been rather dreary. Damp and hunting memorabilia both recurring themes. Things were getting quite disheartening, until I received a message from a lady named Isabel. Isabel owned one of the oldest hotels in town, as well as two rental properties. She and her husband were looking to retire and so she was quite keen to lessen her workload and accept the potential loss in summer rental of Casa Angel. 'Houses are much better if they are lived in!' She told us on our first meeting. As luck would have it Casa Angel was the one Luke and I most liked the look of during our online search, and in real life it didn't disappoint.

It was a beautiful blue wooden house, named after her husband, Angel, who'd grown up in it. Two beds, two bath, open plan kitchen. But it was the front porch that swung it for us. A large cosy sofa, the perfect place to enjoy a glass of wine and stare mesmerised at the property's prime views of the Picos de Europa. We moved in six weeks later, the middle of January 2018.

As part of our relocation Luke and I had set aside some time to really get to know the area and work on our Spanish. And we felt that spending time with El Mexicano fulfilled these aims. We would visit every week or so, and the couple of hours we designated to the visit would inevitably turn into much longer, as we were enlisted in helping with the long list of finca chores. And then, once the day was done, it was expected that we would stay for dinner, which never took less than two hours to prepare. We would eventually make it home well past dark, but always with a bottle of milk, a dozen eggs (even though by this point we'd our own little flock) and on another occasion a cart full of well-rotted cow manure for our first vegetable patch.

Back at our rental, Luke had been allocated a small section of our landlord's field to build a veggie garden. Having grown up in a family of green fingers, with a vegetable patch at the end of their garden and an allotment around the corner from the house, Luke was a dab hand at planning and planting up the vegetable patch. The garden at his family home was long and rectangular, a tangle of annuals, perennials, herbaceous shrubs and fruit trees lovingly tended by his mum, just like how I imagined *The Secret Garden* by Frances Hodgson Burnett would have looked. Luke's mum was a guerrilla gardener, and she'd free sow crocuses and snow drops into the lawn, much to his dad's annoyance when it then came to mowing time. But these mows were irregular, and overall, it'd been a garden for wildlife. By the time Luke moved out he'd added four ponds, to further hinder his dad's mowing attempts.

I, on the other hand, grew up without much involvement in the planting and sowing process, but I did get to enjoy the produce at the end. At my family home there'd been fruiting apple and plum trees at the end of the garden, but otherwise, apart from trees and shrubs around the garden, the lawn was kept quite manicured. Our mowing schedule was much more regular. It was from my grandparents, who conveniently lived next door, where we got to reap the rewards of a productive vegetable garden. Gluts of rhubarb, and asparagus prongs as thick as two fingers in spring. Tomatoes and endless raspberries and blackberries in the summer. Butternut squash, potatoes, onions, courgettes, as well as all the other usual suspects. As a child I remember walking home after an afternoon collecting goodies, and knowing how privileged I was to be picking my food fresh from the ground.

And so, as a priority arriving in Asturias, we had both been keen to cultivate a little plot for ourselves, and it was for this we needed manure. One day whilst sat having coffee at El Mexicano's, Luke spotted that the neighbour's barn was full of cows being kept in over the winter months. And below the stalls was a huge pile of cow poop. Luke asked if he could have some, and the neighbour was delighted to have it taken off his hands. El Mexicano kindly offered Spartacus and his cart to make the delivery. It was only on turning up to load the cart that I realised it was me who was expected to make the journey with Spartacus. But going on previous experience, that shouldn't really have come as a surprise.

I led Spartacus on foot the five miles between El Mexicano's house and ours, sufficiently road safe, the fail-safe red French knickers swinging from the back of the cart. Meanwhile, Luke went ahead to finish preparing the garden for the delivery. I would have been very happy to pootle the journey at a leisurely pace, however, this was not El Mexicano's plan. He followed me the whole distance in his little white Peugeot, waving a great big stick to keep the horse at a trot and me at a brisk jog. I was exhausted. The most recent regular exercise I'd done was a short jog the 400m or so into town, and perhaps a further 800m along the river, that always ended up with me meeting Luke at the bar for a rehydrating beer.

At one point El Mexicano overtook me, and I hoped he'd given up. I maintained my jog while I still believed he could see me in his rearview mirror, but just as I went to slow down, I tripped and fell hard on the tarmac road. The incredible Spartacus jumped to his right and I instinctively rolled to my left, just as the cart full of crap rolled inches from my shoulder. Spartacus came to a stop and waited for me to right myself. My hands were grazed but I came away remarkably lightly. I continued slowly and spied El Mexicano pulled up just around the bend. 'No más!' I said firmly, as I saw him ready his stick to give Spartacus a slap on the bum.

We made it to our rental two hours later, and an hour later the cart was empty just as the sun was beginning to set. El Mexicano pulled the red knickers from his pocket, re-attached them to the back of the cart and motioned for me to climb up into the now empty cart. Thankfully this time El Mexicano did not follow me waving a stick, but I did have to take most of it at a trot for the sun was setting, and it didn't seem the most sensible decision that my first go at driving a horse and cart should take place in the dark. Just when the light had all but gone Luke arrived with a high-vis jacket for me, and he drove behind me for the last half an hour with his lights on full. The red French knickers, as expected, added no extra visibility.

Fortunately, the manure delivered from that trip was enough, and I didn't have to repeat that experience. But our next visit to El Mexicano resulted in yet another gift that caused an ongoing rollercoaster, an orphaned goat kid, who we named Pan.

I really tried to put my foot down when it came to adopting Pan. We were now the proud owners of ten chickens. Luke had grown up with chickens and I'd been taken with the idea of daily fresh eggs and so had easily given my seal of approval to them. We'd added to the pair El Mexicano had gifted us five indistinguishable brown hens, and three even more indistinguishable meat birds. The hens became known as 'the Big Mamas' and the meat chickens 'the Lurches', and they quickly transformed from cage bound creatures (chicken welfare at the ferretería they'd come from, left a lot to be desired) to a confident, companionable crew of chooks. As well as the small square for the vegetable plot, our landlords had allowed us use of their back field. Another small plot of land with four cherry trees in it. Perfect for our chicken numbers, but no great space for a goat.

We first met Pan just before going away for ten days on a work trip to Norway. He was, as goat kids of that age inevitably are, the cutest creature in existence. And we agreed that he could come live with us on our return. But during the trip we'd done some rational thinking and realised that perhaps adopting a goat wasn't the best idea. When we made it home I left it up to Luke to break the news to El Mexicano, whilst I stayed home to catch up on some work. Luke returned later that evening, opened the door and a bolt of white-grey shot past him leaping high off the ground and skipping straight to me. Sending Luke alone had been a terrible mistake, and that is how Pan moved in.

Pan was our introduction to 'livestock keeping', although livestock perhaps wasn't the most accurate term for Pan. Certainly, in those early weeks, when he slept at the end of our bed like a puppy. As the weeks passed, we realised this was getting a bit ridiculous, but we were loath to move him in with the chickens alone. And so, we put word out for a companion goat and were soon offered a little female who'd just been weaned. We named her Coco. Pan wasn't very interested in her to begin with, she was after all a goat, and he was not. Nevertheless, after a couple of days the pair became inseparable. But as anticipated that back field was not big enough for them, and despite our daily walks to offer them more varied forage, we knew it was time for us to make a decision.

Our animal commitments had raised a fair few eyebrows from friends and family back home. 'What are you going to do with them all when you move back to England?' many asked. But we'd known pretty quickly after arriving that we'd found a place we wanted to call home. Spending time with El Mexicano on his finca had only made that clearer for us. We wanted something like that, and what was more, we could achieve it here in Asturias. And so, the search had begun.

Chapter 3

The Story of the Wolf

The small south facing plot that our landlords had allocated us began to transform with four beds carved into the ground filled with the manure collected from El Mexicano's. Unfortunately, the garlic bed was a failure from the beginning, as we learnt too late how wet the ground was and subsequently had to dig a ditch around the whole plot to divert the rains when they came. But the leeks and lettuce that subsequently went in, benefited from the lesson learnt. Raspberry canes were added shortly after. We had a way to go before we would be anywhere near self-sufficient, and so until the time came we relied on our local supermarket. It was there that we first came across the bumper sticker on a family estate parked up outside. The silhouette of a wolf, howling over the carcass of a sheep. The slogan below read 'Con lobos no hay Paraiso' (with wolves there is no paradise).

Luke and I were keen to find a story close to our new home that we could document. We'd been together for four years at this point, after meeting whilst both working in the South Luangwa National Park, in Zambia. He'd been an in-house wildlife photographer and cameraman, for the same company where I was working as a bush camp manager. From there we'd gone on to work together. He still was a wildlife photographer and cameraman; I was writing the stories that accompanied his imagery now. Together we'd find wildlife stories from around the world, from conservation projects to tales of urban wildlife, documenting them for magazines, hotels, production companies and tourist boards. Our first story together had been about an urban peregrine pair who'd nested in the flower box on the balcony of a flat on the twenty-eighth floor of a high rise in Chicago. Their backdrop: that iconic Chicago skyline. The story went viral and a year later we were back, this time filming 'the Perry's' for a BBC Natural World programme. We'd covered so many amazing stories since then and were always looking for the next one.

While Asturias boasted its fair share of exciting wildlife to choose from, the species that hooked us from the start was the Iberian Wolf. A fleeting glimpse of grey fur in the Chernobyl Exclusion Zone, and for Luke a brief encounter in the Bialowiesza forest in Poland, brought our combined total wolf sightings to around twelve seconds.

Now we were chasing our first sighting of an Iberian Wolf. Endemic to the Iberian Peninsula and as good as in our new backyard. As soon as we moved in, we began enquiring about people who might be able to help us. But what we weren't aware of, when we first started out, was how sensitive the subject of the wolf was. And we hadn't expected our first opportunity to potentially see an Iberian Wolf to be at a wolf hunt. Even more bafflingly, at a government organised wolf hunt. We had been tipped off about it by a couple who worked as park rangers, and who wanted to expose the situation.

Once connected the couple had invited us round for lunch at their beautiful home in the Cantabrian mountains. Sat beside a roaring fire in a cosy living room, while the husband prepared lunch, we sat and chatted with the wife, Mila. I wanted to get straight to the wolves, but I could tell Mila was a little hesitant. She wanted to get to know us a bit better, work out if she could trust us.

We ate an amazing meal, drank wine and conversation never faltered, but it was only towards the end of the meal that chat finally turned to the situation with the wolf. Mila hadn't always been such a strong advocate of the wolf; her specialties were in butterflies and orchids. But then, one day, a photo started circulating of a group of men posing with five dead wolves, and the couple were sure that it was an illegal killing. They began looking into it and found out that the cuadrilla (the local hunting group) had been given a permit to kill one wolf, not the five that the photo showed. The mistake the hunters made was that the photo was taken in front of a particularly characteristic old English Oak tree. It took the pair a couple of weeks, but they eventually found the oak tree, and under a bush, not far from the tree, they found the bodies of the five wolves. It was a whole pack.

Mila went on to tell us that despite the photographic evidence, the bodies, and the fact they'd been able to work out exactly who the cuadrilla were, thanks to knowing the group that hunted in that area on that particular day, no criminal charges had yet been formally charged, and the punishment was repeatedly being reduced on appeal. One of the hunters, employed as a wildlife crime police officer, still worked as a wildlife crime police officer.

When the food was cleared away it appeared we'd passed the test, as Mila went into a back room and reappeared with a pile of paperwork. There must have been a few hundred sheets of paper in that pile, and they were all permits to kill wolves.

One request read that a sheep farmer believed that his sheep were being worried by wolves. No sheep had been killed, he hadn't seen a wolf, he had no proof, he just believed it to be wolves. And the response was a permit for him to kill one wolf. She pulled out another sheet of paper. A permit to shoot one wolf, but the two rangers that were at the hunt reported completely different wolves killed. One reported it was a male shot in the shoulder, and the other reported it was a female shot in the stomach.

Five hundred permits were being issued a year to kill wolves, and this was only what was being legally issued. Mila believed that at least five hundred more were being illegally killed. They told us that the previous year, where we now lived, two dead wolves had been found stuffed under a car in the supermarket car park (the same car park where we had first seen the bumper sticker). And another dead wolf strung up on the signpost to a neighbouring town.

At the time there were no records of how many wolves were left in the wild, but Mila and her husband estimated there to be around two thousand. If the couple were right, and a thousand were being killed a year, then you didn't need to be a mathematician to work out that at this rate wolves would soon be extinct.

The couple were part of a group in the process of gathering evidence to take the National Park to court, and to make wolf hunting illegal in Cantabria, actions viewed as a conflict with their jobs as park rangers. They were risking their jobs further by letting us know about the wolf hunts, they did so in the hope that we might be able to shed some light on the goings on.

In preparation of us attending our first legal wolf hunt they explained that there were three ways to hunt wolves. The first, the long wait. A hide would be set up, area baited, and you then waited until a wolf showed up. And then you shot it. As ways went, this one seemed pretty civilised. The second, the traditional hunt. During hunting season (for deer and boar) you were given a permit to, if spotted, kill a wolf during the hunt. And the third type was a hunt where members of the public and government employees came together, en masse, to drive wolves down a valley, using dogs and explosives, into a line of guns. It was the third way that we were tipped off about.

Now these events weren't well publicised. Those in the know were usually the villagers who'd called for the removal of the wolf, and the government employees, from highway maintenance men to park rangers, who are tasked with the role of flushing out the wolves. Information about a hunt like this was treated very delicately. The phone rang one April evening, to let us know that it would be taking place early the very next day, in the region of Mazcuerras.

Chapter 4

We're Going on a Wolf Hunt

On the day of the wolf hunt we woke at four thirty in the morning to thick fog, and with the weather reports telling us that it wasn't set to lift until midday we were certain that the hunt would surely be called off. But with no other plans for the day we headed off anyway, just in case. We'd been given two locations; the first was where we should leave the car, at a nearby restaurant, and the second was the best place to use as a viewpoint.

When we arrived twenty odd 4x4s, including two Park Ranger vehicles, were already at the restaurant, and so I told Luke to keep driving. Apparently, the wolf hunters had the same idea as us and were currently rendezvousing where we were about to park our car.

'Well, at least we know we've come to the right place!' Luke said, but I could tell he was as nervous as I was. We made a plan to park as we intended and start walking to the viewpoint. We were in an English car, and really there was no reason for them to see us as anything other than tourists. We turned around just in time to see a convoy of 4x4s heading off. Luckily, we were just in time to see the direction they were headed in so once we'd parked the car, we set off on foot in their wake.

The route took us through a beautiful oak wood. A Pied Flycatcher flitted about, woodpeckers called, and we even saw a couple of Cuckoos roll through the canopy, newly arrived from Africa. At the end of the wood we popped out into a steep meadow where Woodlarks were in full mating display. Flying upwards before parachuting down into the heath, singing their melodious warbling song as they descended. A smart male Stonechat stood proudly atop a fence post, hopping forward every other one as we reached him. If it wasn't for the fact that we were there for a wolf hunt, this was turning out to be a glorious morning's birding.

The valley below was still carpeted in fog. Sun beams cut through the pines, but the mist began to burn off and the peaks of the mountains, which reached for miles out ahead of us, were now visible. We climbed a fair distance but after almost an hour of walking we were still no closer to the viewpoint, and we hadn't seen any of the cars from earlier. Being on foot we were at a distinct disadvantage, and we passed numerous turn offs that the group could well have taken. But we decided that our best chance was to continue towards the viewpoint co-ordinates we'd originally been tipped off about.

The road curled back on itself and that was when we spotted our first hunter. Despite the road being a public right of way a navy 4x4 straddled the path and the verge, a rifle lent up against the back door, and the fifty-something-year-old man that stood beside it seemed surprised to see us. Luke and I stopped for a moment, looked through our binoculars, and then we continued, smiling sweetly as we passed. Our greeting of 'hola' was met with a stony stare. The hunting season finished 1 February, and it was now late April. The wolf hunt was definitely on.

The road curled back on itself once more until we were directly above the gunman and at the far end of the road we spotted our second 4x4. Our second hunter suddenly appeared in the bracken beneath us. Unlike the other man, he was wearing an orange reflective jacket. He eyeballed us and began to walk towards us, but we continued leisurely on our way and had he meant to approach us he never did.

Around the corner the valley opened into a bowl, and we spotted three more guns forming a circle around the top edge. We'd found the line of guns.

Just as we were deliberating where to position ourselves, the morning's chorus of birdsong was obliterated as explosions began from the direction of where we'd parked the car. As the rumble of explosives increased it didn't take long to work out the hunt's tactics. They were forcing all the animals up the hill and to the bowl. So, we took a seat above the final gunman and began to wait and watch. A flock of Yellow Wagtails bobbed amongst a small herd of cattle, a Ring Ouzel sat atop a solitary tree. All very idyllic, ignoring the gunmen scattered beneath us, and the explosions edging ever closer to us from the valley below.

For two hours the explosions crept closer and closer, and gradually the gunmen went from relaxed and reclining against the trees, to upright and alert.

Three deer exploded out of the bushes, the gunman below us raised his gun but managed to steady himself and refrain from pulling the trigger. The deer were not his intended quarry. If a wolf was to appear in the spot the deer had, it didn't stand a chance.

What amazed us was not only that this was happening, but that it was happening in spring, probably the most delicate time for an ecosystem. Tired, newly arrived migrant birds were feeding up, others nesting. Mammals would be giving birth or denning in the forest that was now being flushed by people, banging against the trees and bushes, and setting off fireworks. After one explosion a Hobby alighted from the forest.

Finally, we could see the smoke from the explosives being used, the cattle now running away in terror. By now walkers, runners and cyclists were using the road that Luke and I were sat on. The same road that ran alongside the bowl that the strategically placed guns were sat within.

At around 11 a.m. the first explosive throwers, wearing their luminescent jackets, appeared on the tree line, and we watched as they lit what looked like sticks of dynamite and threw them into any nearby bush or dense scrub. A few seconds pause, then an almighty explosion and a puff of blue smoke followed by the smell of burnt gunpowder. The beaters reached the guns, and the hunt was declared over.

Once the hunting group dispersed, Luke and I made our way back down and drove over to the neighbouring town to meet Mila, who'd tipped us off, for a drink. The chosen spot was where the hunters were known to gather after a hunt, to show off what they'd shot that day. So, if they had killed a wolf today, then it was very likely we would see it there.

Mila asked how we were feeling, and there was only one word for it: shock. We just couldn't understand how they could do this in the middle of spring, it being peak nesting and denning time for all wildlife. They told us that the week before the hunt had scared a bear and two cubs out into the line of gunmen. And bears were meant to be protected.

Not long after we arrived, the two rangers' cars, which we'd seen earlier that morning, pulled up and three rangers entered the bar. We peered into the back of their pick-ups, braced for what we might see, but this time their boots were empty.

We did go along to one other wolf hunt, but this time it covered a vastly larger area. And although we came across numerous pockets of men with flags and fireworks, who created a relay of constant explosions down the length of the valley throughout the day, we never did find any guns.

We did have one encounter that made us reconsider whether it was a smart idea for us to be there. We'd taken a scrubby forest track that led through a pine forest, and headed to what we hoped was the peak of a ridge that cut across the valley. On reaching the crest and realising it did not offer the view we anticipated, we turned back to find our English plated car surrounded by a group of ten or so men. They were wearing khakis and carrying walkie talkies and bundles of explosives. Nervously we greeted them. Luke lifted his binoculars to investigate a bird, and then pulled out his *Collins Bird Guide*. We were nothing more than two English birdwatchers. One of the men asked to try Luke's binoculars, and he obliged. The man was impressed and passed them to his friend. This went on as every member of the group had a go, and all the while explosions continued from every direction.

Several silhouettes appeared on the rocky escarpment across the valley from us, and white flashes and puffs of smoke preceded more blasts. From the cliffs below the figures thirty or so Griffon Vultures took flight, disturbed from their breeding colony. The men pointed to each other and turned our borrowed binoculars on the birds. A crackle on their radios notified them that it was time to begin their leg of the beat, and they handed back the binoculars and bid us farewell. The familiar hiss, then boom and cloud of smoke soon erupted from the group that just left.

Although most of the group were good natured with us, there were a few who seemed distrustful. We both admitted afterwards that the encounter had left us feeling nervous. On top of this, a scrawled 'vivo lobos' had recently appeared on the underpass near our local town and Jack, a new friend whose Airbnb we'd stayed in during our very first visit to the area, had joked that he thought it might have been us who'd made the graffiti, despite the fact that we'd been away when it appeared. He warned us that if anyone truly believed it was us we would need to be careful. It was becoming clear that the wolf situation was not only more complex than we could have imagined, but also potentially dangerous. Despite receiving more tip-offs to these hunts, we decided not to attend another.

Chapter 5

When the Broom Flowers

The mountains were ablaze with purple heather and yellow broom as we set off up the steep mountain track. We were out of breath within seconds of starting off, but Pablo, our guide for the next two days, was patient, and he stopped often to let us rest. 'It is said that when the broom flowers, the wolf is born,' he told us. Pablo was a biologist for the government, and he'd spent the past twenty years studying the Iberian Wolf. That day he was taking us to observe a wolf den that he knew well, one that he'd been observing almost weekly for the past five years. 'You really can't tell anyone about this site,' he briefed us. Two years ago, a pack of wolves had denned near the road we'd just driven up, and a walker had come across them. The following day people from the local village returned to the spot, killed the four pups and then waited for the pack to return and shot every last one of them. Pablo needn't have worried; our lips were sealed.

It wasn't our first meeting with Pablo. Our first meeting was more of an interview, a coffee in a city, far from Pablo's natural environment. It'd been Mila that'd introduced us, and like them, Pablo had also needed to check us out before sharing his knowledge.

The mountains rose and fell dramatically, like rough seas ahead of us, and it was this very landscape that helped preserve this wolf pack. We followed a cow trail along the side of the mountain, trying not to step on the orchids that peppered the route. The cows' bells chimed as the free-roaming cows grazed and a Montagu's Harrier hunted nearby. Although struggling in the plains, due to intensification of agriculture, they were doing surprisingly well in the mountains, Pablo told us. And then there were all the migrants we spotted along the route. A Bluethroat sung in the distance, a Northern Wheatear eyed us as we'd passed.

Finally, just as the temperature began to drop, we made it to our viewing spot. Pablo showed us a film on his phone from the week before, of two bears grazing in the exact position we were now sitting.

Scanning the opposite hillside for movement the odd spooked deer caught our eye, but as the sun began to set there was still no sign of our target. We watched as the horses and cows gathered altogether for the night ahead. Learnt behaviour from living in wolf territory, Pablo pointed out to us. Eventually when there was no longer light enough to see through our binoculars, we called it a day.

Pablo found a relatively flat area and we unrolled our sleeping bags under a star strewn sky. After a dinner of cheese and bread, and once settled as comfortably as one can be on a rocky mountainside, Pablo began to howl. It was so wolf like that it gave me shivers. But there was no reply. Pablo tried a few more times, but with no luck. And with each unanswered howl we could tell he was getting worried. Pablo was monitoring quite a few wolf packs, but this was his local one. In fact, at the peak of our climb he'd pointed out his home. He'd checked on them just the week before and they'd been active. But as his earlier story showed, a lot can happen in a week.

'Hopefully they are just out hunting,' Pablo reassured, a comment directed more to himself than us. Wolves can travel up to 20km a day, so it was possible that they were somewhere out of earshot of Pablo's howls. But even though we were in amongst what looked like endless mountains, there were some twinkling lights down the valley. Only a small village, home to about ten or so people, but a stark reminder that humans were never really very far away, even when you thought you were in the wildest of wilds.

Around midnight a storm passed over the adjacent mountains. A fireworks display of lighting and ground shuddering thunder, but fortunately where we lay remained dry. We awoke the next morning to a sky bursting with pink and orange. After rolling up our sleeping bags and shaking off the cold of the hard ground from our bones, we made our way back to our viewing spot.

We watched as the cows and horses dispersed from their nighttime corral, and then... 'Lobo! Down by the fence!' We scanned the direction Pablo was detailing but neither Luke nor I could see it. Pablo got the wolf in his scope and ushered for me to look. I held my breath and closed one eye, directing the other down the lens. It took me a moment to make him out, his fur the perfect camouflage, but when I saw him, he was unmistakable. His pelt was thick and tawny coloured, his eyes focussed, his ears alert. His belly was large and round, a sign of a successful night's hunting.

Pablo identified it as the alpha male. The fact that this alpha male had made it to five or six years old was a miracle, he said. And then two more wolves appeared behind the first.

The alpha male began to move again, making his way towards the area Pablo had pointed out as the den. As quickly as the wolf appeared, he disappeared amongst the scrub. We sat, watched, and waited for the three wolves to reappear. Pablo predicted where they would cross but an hour later there was still no sign of them. They were still there, for terrified Red Deer kept pronking away, only they were so well camouflaged amongst the garrigue. And then, in a small watering hole at the very top of the opposite mountain, I spotted those distinctive ears. It was the alpha male again. The heat and his swollen tummy had got the better of him and he was taking a well-deserved dip. We watched him as he wallowed. After five minutes of indulgence, he began to descend the mountain, lost once more behind the scrub, and then he entered the clearing beside the den site. There the alpha female joined him.

They played and groomed for an hour or so, until finally they entered the den, melting into the rocky outcrop.

'They are phantoms,' Pablo said simply.

As we retraced our steps from the day before, Pablo stopped us. There were fresh wolf tracks over our own, metres from where we'd spent the previous night. The wolves had come to check us out in the night.

Our second night was spent at a different location, and there we enjoyed another wildlife first, the Cantabrian Brown Bear. Despite the bear benefiting from huge conservation efforts in recent years, the bear is another animal with a very complex relationship with humans here in Northern Spain. Pablo explained that thanks to illegal poaching, hunting, and human expansion, the Cantabrian Brown Bear had been pushed to the verge of extinction. At the lowest point their numbers were thought to be just sixty or seventy individuals. They were declared a protected species in 1973, which meant hunting was prohibited, and compensation began to be paid for all livestock and agricultural damages made by the bears. But perhaps the most effective tool to protect the bear was the promotion of bear-watching, which boosted the tourism economy in sleepy towns in the region. At the time there was thought to be between two hundred and fifty, and three hundred bears, but the battle was not yet over. The populations were split into two isolated subpopulations with a low rate of genetic variability and a small number of bears in each, and persecution persisted. Whether farmers or 'accidental' killings during the hunting season were the cause, ever since we'd first moved to the area there'd been quite a few reports of dead bears at the hands of humans.

However, that evening, we got to observe two bears grazing on the opposite mountainside to where we sat, one male and one female. The sound of toppling rocks had given them away. It was a nondescript sound to Luke and me, but to Pablo it was the sound of a bear looking under stones for grubs and other yummy morsels. Sure enough, twenty minutes after Pablo alerted us to the sound our first bear emerged into a clear patch. And not long after that, a second appeared. We watched them ambling about their business, in that uniquely bear-like manner, for two hours until we lost the light. We spent the night a little further up the mountain in a stone refuge beside a roaring fire. And when we left the next morning, we missed crossing paths with a bear by moments. The steaming bear poo that sat hot and wet just outside the door was the giveaway to its passing.

Chapter 6

El Chorco de los Lobos

It was time to get a new car. We could only legally have Luke's English car in Spain for six months, plus we were also spending a lot of time in the mountains and felt that a bigger car, better suited to this terrain, was a sensible move. It would have to be second hand, although second-hand cars were shockingly expensive still, and we finally settled on an old Suzuki Vitara. It was nearly thirty years old and it looked it, but it had character, fitted in nicely with all the local farmers, and wouldn't have looked out of place with a 'Con lobos no hay Paraiso' sticker on the bumper. My Granny named our new/old car the Skidonk, as that was what they called very old cars in Zambia, where she lived.

Perhaps unsurprisingly, only a month after we'd bought it, the Skidonk was coughing up oil, jarring into and jumping out of gears, and so we'd returned to the dealer we'd bought it from, for help. Fortunately, we still had the English car, and while Luke went ahead in the Skidonk, I'd followed. Waiting in the car, I watched as Luke explained to the mechanic the issues. It all looked relatively straightforward, and then the mechanic had lifted the arm of his shirt to show Luke something I couldn't quite make out, which threw me a bit.

Half an hour later he returned to the car. 'Did you know that the mechanic has a massive wolf tattoo on his upper arm?' 'No, I didn't,' I replied. 'Not sure when I would have seen him without his top off.' Luke ignored my quip. 'Yeh and he loves wolves! Even though they did kill seven of his sheep in one night.' Well, that explained the half hour. After describing the Skidonk's ailments, and why we needed it back up and running at full capacity, namely for our trips to the mountains to film

28

wolves, the mechanic had replied by rolling up his sleeve to reveal the face of a wolf. It was refreshing for Luke to chat to someone who was pro-wolf, for in the past weeks there had been numerous anti-wolf demonstrations. One particularly large demonstration took place in Cabrales, a village only a twenty-minute drive from our own, and world renowned for its cheese. But the Cabrales cheese is more than a simple dairy product, it is their identity. And for as long as they have been making cheese, they have been hating wolves.

The news reported that five hundred farmers and shepherds met that day to protest the increasing number of livestock killings. Killings they believed were committed by wolves. The day after the demonstration, the decapitated head of a wolf was found in a public swimming pool in a neighbouring town.

At the bottom of the hill from our rental was a ferretería, a sort of hardware shop that fulfilled much of your typical DIY and self-sufficient living needs. The proprietor of our local ferretería was a very friendly man named Felipo. Since our first visit there Felipo took an interest in us and our purchases. We'd bought our first five chickens from him, vegetables for the garden, nails for fencing and so forth. He didn't judge our beginner Spanish, but always encouraged us to talk more, and one of his favourite topics to debate with Luke was the situation with the wolf. Felipo had no reservations in sharing how much he hated them.

For Felipo the wolves belonged in the mountains, and if they would just stay up there then it would be fine. But they didn't, they would come into the villages where they didn't belong and kill livestock that wasn't theirs to kill. Felipo knew who'd killed the two wolves found in the supermarket car park, and the one found hanging from the road sign. The last time we were in there he'd told Luke about a lone wolf which was hanging around the neighbouring town. Likely the same one who's head was found in the swimming pool.

After our time spent with Pablo, we were eager to start filming some natural history footage of the wolves. But first we needed to get our filming and photography permits. We'd applied to the four separate boards (Asturias, Cantabria, Castilla y Leon and the Picos de Europa) at the beginning of spring. Legally they were supposed to reply within a month of receiving the applications, but two months later we still hadn't heard anything. Finally, Pablo called on our behalf to find out the status of our applications, and a month later we received permits for three out of the four locations. All for a year, but all back dated to the date we first applied for them, and with the prerequisite that we were expected to give ten days' notice before we did any filming. Not only did we lose three months of filming, we also couldn't be reactive if situations were to arise thanks to the required notice period.

By this time, we'd already made the decision to take a step back from the story of the wolf. As well as the story being as complex as it was, the hurdles to get permits had proven that we were going to struggle to get access to the whole story. We'd also decided that we wanted to make our home here. Upsetting anyone at this stage would have been foolish. But even if we didn't end up telling the story, we still wanted to understand as much as we could about the situation. And so, we decided to take a few days and venture into the Picos, just to see what we could learn for ourselves.

To go looking for wolves without a local guide, or local knowledge, was proving to be a needle in the haystack sort of scenario. But I'd been told about a place called El Chorco de los Lobos, which directly translates as 'The Choke of the Wolves'. Up until as recently as 1950 this location had been used to capture what was regarded as the 'top predator of the cattle herd'.

During the winter, when much of the upper areas of the valley in the territory of Valdeón remained covered in snow, the wolf would come down to the forests and meadows below to hunt. The same place where the cattle were grazed during those cold winter months. It is said that at the beginning of the sixteenth century there were so many wolves that the Valdeón Valley cattle were decimated. And so, on Mount Corona, between the towns of Cordiñanes de Valdeón and Caín, right next to the road that connects these towns, El Chorco de los Lobos was built.

With the area being so geographically isolated, El Chorco de los Lobos became an important point of union for the surrounding towns. It held such importance for the local community that rules were written from its initiation, which stated how exactly the wolf was to be captured, the positions and functions expected from each participant, and the obligations for maintaining the site. The oldest legislation of the regulations for El Chorco de los Lobos dates from 1610, with a reform made in 1776 which declared who exactly could participate in the wolf hunts: heads of the family, men over 16 years of age and under 65, service servants, and/or the most useful people in each house. And if there weren't any, only then could the women be involved.

The hunts took place any day of the year, at any time, except when Holy Mass was being celebrated. Notice for participants to gather was a specific ringing of the bell at the Church of Sta. Eulalia in Posada de Valdeón. If it was agreed that a hunt was necessary then the Huntsman from Posada would notify the Huntsman from Soto, and the Huntsman from Soto would notify the Huntsman from Caldevilla. The tourist write-up of El Chorco de los Lobos called it an 'Ethnographic heritage with 400 years of history'. It seemed as good a place as any to try and begin to understand the local attitude to the wolf.

En route to El Chorco de los Lobos we made a stop at a refugio called Vegabaño, which lay above the forest of Soto de Sajambre. The forest was something from a Grimm's fairytale, dripping with lichen and cloaked in an ethereal blanket of mist. But above the forest, where the refugio lay, was a meadow, grazed to the very roots. We live in a confusing time where overgrazed landscapes are considered beautiful. Clean. Paradise.

I mention this stop, not just for the fact it has the possibility of being the most idyllic natural utopia, but also because that evening at dinner we met a couple. A Brit and an Aussie, both now living in Brighton. It was their last night in the Picos, and we talked about the walking route they'd taken, and what they'd seen along the way. They had seen many Fire Salamanders, which made us green with envy, as we had yet to see any of these mythical-looking creatures. Black with yellow splodges, their name comes from the old belief that they were born in fire. This legend likely arose from the fact that Fire Salamanders hibernate in hollow logs. When people gathered these logs to build a fire, they reportedly saw the salamanders emerging from the flames.

And then we asked if they'd seen any wolves. Here the conversation got a bit sticky. To begin with they hadn't even known there were wolves in Spain, let alone the mountains they'd spent the past ten days hiking. This didn't surprise me. Most people, even those who have a passion for wildlife, are always shocked to hear there are still wolves here. We voiced what a shame we thought it was that the wolves weren't championed, for their presence could surely bring in a huge increase in wildlife tourism. Instead, the wolf was being actively persecuted, seemingly without retribution against those responsible. But I could tell that they didn't feel it was our place to have an opinion on this matter. 'Surely this is a local issue,' one of the ladies neatly suggested.

I agreed with her, of course it was a local issue. And I'd explained how we were collaborating with local rangers, a government biologist, some local wildlife guides, in our endeavour to understand the story. But after that the conversation petered out. They clearly felt that it was not our place to have an opinion, or tell the story, irrelevant of who we were collaborating with. We were foreigners, and so we didn't get a say.

The next morning, we set out for El Chorco de los Lobos. The towering peaks at the upper end of the Valdeon Valley stood like geological cathedrals. Clouds scudded overhead, grazing the jagged rock tops and occasionally revealing glimpses of cerulean blue, where vultures glided on the thermals. As the rock walls softened, the slopes became carpeted with beech trees. The Cares River emerges, bubbling down the valley, leaping over water-worn rocks, and splashing into azure pools. It is a breathtakingly beautiful spot, where I can imagine wolves sauntering through. But if they roam today, it will be when no human eyes are watching. In these parts, their reputation is one of death and destruction, a legacy of livestock obliteration. In payment for their reign of terror, a place of nightmares has been erected for the wolves. In the shadow of Monte Corona, the beech forests tumble their way to the road, a natural tunnel of foliage as the trees reach out to each other, almost touching overhead. Away from the sun there is a damp eerie coolness, not dissimilar to the feeling you get in an old graveyard. And this is the entrance to El Chorco de los Lobos, where the hunt of the wolf has been immortalised.

The trap is a V shape, the widest part at the top of a steep slope, which rolls down towards the river. The sides have been created using both natural and manmade forms. Gnarled trees and natural rock, and what look like small one-man wooden boats, cut in half and placed with the pointy end sticking up. Inside the hollowed-out wood there are seats for the men to sit and wait for a wolf to be driven downwards, to the bottom of the V. The funnel continues to narrow until it finishes in a tunnel that seemingly disappears into nothing.

I put myself in the wolf's paws. Being chased down the mountainside. Crashes and bangs, smoke and fire forcing your route. Stones rain down, shouts from behind strange structures.

A stone cracks at your side, you turn to run but an impenetrable barrier blocks your way. Behind you more stones hail down, more noise, more fear. You follow the only route open to you. A hole appears ahead. You run for it, and then you are falling. Smooth rock stops your descent, a cave with no exit. And then the stones begin to hail down, sticks striking from above. The hunter most hunted, the killer most killed.

Chapter 7

Not Plains Ready

Whilst at El Chorco de los Lobos, Pablo was sending us details of a beautiful walk close by that took you to the top of a peak which offered stunning views of the lake. It was also a site that was confirmed to have wolves denning, and apparently the pack was being seen regularly.

The track started gently; hundreds of crickets flashed a brilliant blue as they jumped out of our way. We spotted huge paw prints, but it was hard to tell it they were wolf or Spanish Mastiff, the region's guardian dogs bred to protect livestock from the wolves, known locally as mastíns. After about an hour the route began to curve upwards and the going got tougher, even more so in the ever-increasing heat. Fortunately, the route led us into an old forest which was much cooler and easier going. Branches crashed to our left as our entrance into the wood scared a couple of Roe Deer. Red Deer droppings and Wild Boar diggings confirmed that there was certainly prey for the wolves.

Suddenly the path disappeared, something that hadn't been noted in the directions, and so we free-styled our way to the crest of the hill, where we found a herd of goats accompanied by a mastín. It approached us barking threateningly and we reached for a rock, as Pablo had told us to do if we ever found ourselves in this position. Spanish mastíns are known to sometimes be quite combative, seeing any stranger as a threat to their charges. We spotted a peak that we guessed must be the peak Pablo meant, and headed off in its direction, the mastín backing off now that he knew his goat family was safe.

The peak was rocky and in parts required more climbing than we anticipated, but we made it to the top. Luke held up the photo Pablo had sent, showing the views from the top, only to realise it didn't match our current view. We were standing on the wrong peak. Behind us rose a much taller peak, the one Pablo actually meant. It turned out that we'd taken a wrong turn right at the start of the route, back in the village.

There was no sighting of wolves that day but as we made our way back down, we came across sure proof that wolves were around. A giant wolf poo, packed with hair, sat in the middle of the track. Following Pablo's lead, we kicked it off the road and into the bushes. You didn't want the wrong person finding out the wolves were around. Although from what we'd been told it seemed that most people already knew. After all, they weren't far from the village we were parked in.

On our drive home that evening we found ourselves ravenous, our snack bag forgotten in the boot of the car. Along the road from Riaño to our neighbouring town there are very few places to pull over, for the road winds through the narrowest of gorges. But we finally found a spot, just outside a house, where we could quickly park up and grab said bag. As soon as the car stopped a little old lady came out of the house and was already leaning against my open window, chatting away to Luke, by the time I'd retrieved the snacks from the boot.

Lovely weather, she observed. It was a very British way to begin a conversation.

'Not back there,' Luke replied, for we'd driven through some impressive rain which'd appeared out of nowhere.

Oh, she was expecting rain, she told us. They used to never have the mist or much rain, but since the lake was flooded, they got much more, she went on. Riaño Lake was in fact a reservoir, made in the 1980s for flood control, and to generate hydroelectric power. Old Riaño and six other villages were submerged as a result of the dam project, and New Riaño re-built above the reservoir waters.

She was intrigued to see two young English people, and even more intrigued to learn that we now lived here. We talked about the food. Much better than England, she informed us. According to her all we ate in England was McDonalds. She then went on to scold us, our Spanish should be a lot better considering how long we'd now been in Spain! Poor Luke was holding the majority of the conversation, and I thought he was doing very well. So, he steered the conversation to a topic he felt more confident conversing in Spanish about, wildlife, and of course, this led ultimately to wolves.

The old woman shook her head when he mentioned 'lobos'. Here all the time, she muttered, gesturing a hand to the land that rose sharply up from the other side of the road. Always taking the sheep.

She didn't believe that the wolves should be completely wiped out, but she was adamant that there were too many. And then her monologue on the situation began to echo that of a park ranger from Ponga, who we'd met in the early days of moving to the area. The wolves weren't always here, and now they've come back, and the farmers have never had to deal with them in this way. The park ranger had said the same sort of thing. In the areas that there'd always been wolves the local people knew how to deal with them, but in the villages where the wolves had been extirpated and people hadn't had to live with them in recent memory, to have them coming back was a problem. These people were angry and didn't believe the wolves belonged there.

Even more interesting was that the old woman also agreed with the park ranger on the measures being taken to control the wolves, that they weren't working. The three states of Asturias, Cantabria and Castilla y Leon, all prescribed very different rules on how to manage wolves. But ultimately in all three states, whether legally or illegally, it seemed that only the odd wolf here and there was being culled/killed/controlled. And herein lay one of the problems with the methodology, perhaps. Picking off wolves here and there weakened a pack, and weak packs did not go for strong prey. They targeted easy prey. They targeted livestock. And unlike in the area we had visited with Pablo, where we had watched the livestock come together at nightfall for, they knew how to take precautions against the wolves they shared the landscape with, here the livestock hadn't learned to live with wolves, making them even easier prey.

The conversation reminded me of a story I'd been told about a private safari collection in South Africa where they'd bought a herd of thirty wildebeest. Only the wildebeest had previously been part of a collection where there were no predators. So, when the wildebeest were introduced to their new home, and the pride of lions found them, it was a blood bath. Only three wildebeest survived the onslaught. The person telling me the story explained the wildebeest weren't 'plains ready'. In the areas here in Spain, where the wolves were re-colonising, the domesticated cattle, sheep and goats were the same as the wildebeest. They weren't 'plains ready', and therefore they didn't stand a chance. In the areas where there had always been wolves, the livestock were put with mastíns, and as seen with Pablo, the livestock learnt to congregate when night fell. But in the areas where wolves were returning, the local farmers still believed they could leave their animals up in the mountains unattended, and those very animals were proving that they weren't 'plains ready'.

Chapter 8

Wild Finca

It may not have been wolf damage we were facing, but back at our rental we were currently facing another mammal onslaught. The landlord's donkeys and sheep kept breaking into our little vegetable patch. Cabbages, pumpkins, raspberries, spinach, all our greens gone. Only the onions they'd turned their noses up to. We'd been devastated, and the loss of our little veg garden only confirmed what we already knew, that we needed to find ourselves a home of our own.

We'd asked El Mexicano if he might know of anywhere, and immediately he said he knew of just the place. He had a distant cousin that lived next door to a dilapidated old dairy farm that was for sale. We'd seen the property online, but the photos were awful, and so we'd scrolled past it quite a few times during our day-dreaming property searches. But El Mexicano insisted that we needed to see it in person, for he believed it fulfilled everything we were looking for. And so, it was thanks to El Mexicano that, at the beginning of the summer of 2018, we first laid eyes on Wild Finca.

We followed El Mexicano up the hill from town, the road was neither too windy nor too narrow, through the little village to where the road ended beside a pretty little stone fuente. A green path continued beyond the fuente, whilst right took us down a steep driveway, Picu Moru rose ahead of us. At the bottom of the driveway it forked, to the right was El Mexicano's distant cousin, to the left, a driveway lined in Early Purple Orchids ended at the finca that was for sale. Beyond the buildings rose the Sueve mountains range, which continued into three hundred and sixty degrees of mountains, and yet the nearest land was surprisingly flat before disappearing down into a forest. We were greeted by the owner, an old ganadero. He was a tiny man in all features except for a pair of giant ears, and for this reason he reminded me of Roald Dahl's BFG. He subsequently became named so in Luke's phone. There were a number of buildings that made up the property, all in varying states of decay. The main farmhouse was crumbling and uninhabitable. With rough render the hórreo had been transformed to resemble a little cottage, and this was where the BFG was living and had been for a while it seemed. There were open triangle-shaped holes in the walls stuffed with old animal feedbags to keep out the cold. There was a smaller barn, now collapsing thanks to an impressive walnut tree whose limbs were growing through the roof, and whose roots were coming up through the concrete floor. There were two small grain stores, and the most dependable of all the buildings, a huge cow barn. In his heyday the BFG was an award-winning cattle farmer, and it was clear where his priorities had lain; with his champion herd enjoying a more reliable roof over their head than the BFG himself. The buildings were in fact quite true to the photos we'd seen online. But what hadn't been pictured online, and what sold it for us was the stunning seven hectares of fields, scrub and heath that came with the finca. Even though the property sat tucked away in a valley, the land around the house was remarkably flat. It got sun throughout the day, and it was surrounded by the most stunning views. Down the valley rose the Picos de Europa, directly across the valley towered Picu Moru and, to the northwest, was the Sierra del Sueve. It boasted wildflower meadows, an orchard of apple, plum and other fruit trees I did not know the names of. Plenty of space for a vegetable garden, our chickens and goats, plus the horses and pigs we dreamed of having in the future. There were walking and riding trails straight from the front door, and below us was an extensive woodland of Sweet Chestnut, English Oak and Common Hazel.

There were only a handful of other houses in sight, making it feel both remote and rural, and yet it was also only a seven-minute drive to the local town. The same town we currently lived a five-minute walk from, and the town we'd fallen in love with.

As the BFG walked us around the land Luke asked if he ever saw vultures. The BFG assured us not to worry, there were never any vultures at his farm. (There are some very strange feelings towards the vulture in the area, many still believe the vulture predate livestock, and the BFG was clearly of that ilk.) We were hugely relieved when a large shadow fell over us, and a Griffon Vulture swooped low overhead. The timing felt serendipitous.

What stopped us from making an offer that first visit was the work the buildings required. It was a huge project, one that neither Luke nor I had any experience of. And it was this fact that kept us looking through the summer months.

El Mexicano's son, who kept a yard and trained horses not so far from El Mexicano, took us out riding one day to show us a few farms near him that he guessed were for sale (guessed on the basis that the owners were recently deceased, and with no prospect lined up to take them over). One had potential, accessed via a dirt track through a woodland, the farm sat within a stunning wildflower meadow. The farmhouse was in relatively good condition, certainly liveable, a brand-new tractor parked up in the outbuilding. The owner had only just passed, washing still hung on the line outside. El Mexicano's son put out feelers, but the feedback was that ownership had passed to ten plus family members, some uncontactable, so it would be years before the paperwork would be sorted out. This was another issue we came across on a few occasions, multiple claimants on the older properties tended to complicate things.

The summer of 2018, as well as chasing wolves and looking for our new home, was also the summer I turned thirty. To celebrate, friends came to stay, remarking on how Un-Spain-like

Asturias was. Spain isn't green! And to give them the proper experience of our new home we'd taken on the mighty Sella River, a world-renowned body of water that each year canoe enthusiasts in their thousands came to ride.

The twenty-kilometre route goes from our local town to the nearest beach town, and my family, friends and I managed it in five hours. Perhaps one of the longest descents in history, due to the number of times we had stopped at the chiringuitos set up along the way for a sidra. Sidra in Asturias is somewhat of a religion, and there's a very specific way of drinking it. For starters there is an art to the pour. It must be done from a great height, the higher the distance from bottle exit to glass entry, the more aerated the cider. And then you must drink it all in one go, to ensure it stays fizzy for the duration of consumption.

When my sister, Jemima, first visited, a bartender almost knocked out a tooth in his shock at her taking only a polite sip, he'd tried to force the rest of the sidra down her throat. Originally, we'd wanted everyone to experience the authentic method as a complete surprise, but after Jemima's near miss we decided that perhaps people needed a bit more of a heads up on the protocol. And even then, months later when our friends Katy and Oki had come to visit, and the bartender poured not just one but all four glasses in one go (he had extremely large bear-like hands that somehow balanced perfectly the four sidra glasses) and we'd broken out into applause, his glare told us that that was not a respectful response. Other places only gave you one glass between your group. Learning the correct etiquette for drinking sidra in Asturias was an ongoing lesson for us. But at the chiringuitos we'd been trusted to serve ourselves, and whilst everyone failed miserably at the high pour, most sidra being lost to the river, we were still immeasurably over served. Meaning that despite being some of the first on the river, we'd been the last at the finish line.

To put things into perspective, a month later we watched competitors at the eighty-second Descenso del Sella complete the route in one hour and eighteen minutes. The start was just below our landlady's hotel, and she'd invited us to watch it from one of the hotel balconies. It'd been an incredible mass of bodies and plastic piling into the water. Locals from the town of Infiesto dressed as water nymphs (just one example of the event's eclectic traditions) and danced beneath the bridge as the competitors vied for the best positions on the water. A stream of one and two person canoes, from all over the world, glided past for a good five minutes. Trailed by a few joyriders in inflatable dinghies wearing Hawaiian skirts, large, brimmed hats and drinking cocktails. And with them clear of sight, the party on the banks retreated into town to watch the remainder of the race on TV screens being played at all the bars. During this race, the competitors and supporters witnessed a particularly intriguing twist of events when the fourth placing pair, a local duo, on nearing the finish line, jumped out of their canoe and ran across some mud flats to cut off the leaders. The sneaky manoeuvre snatched them second stand on the podium. The controversy of the tactical move threw a lot of visiting competitors' noses out of joint. Most noticeably the two South Africans they'd pipped to the post, their scowling faces from position three on the podium quite at odds with the rest of the celebrations.

Chapter 9

The Bees

Alongside these summer festivities, Luke surprised me with a very exciting IOU: two bee hives. I'd become a little bit obsessed with honey, one of the reasons being its remarkable healing capacity. Pan was a rather sickly kid, having never received colostrum at birth, and we'd spent those first months back and forth to the vet, who thought we were rather ridiculous bringing a goat to him (when he specialised in cats and dogs). But the livestock vet wouldn't come for just one goat, and so this pet vet ended up being our best option. Plus, Pan and Coco were used to riding around in the back of the Skidonk, so they really were as good as dogs.

One afternoon, while foraging in the spinney behind the rental, Pan returned with a limp. On inspection he had a puncture wound from a bramble thorn, which we thought would heal by itself but instead caused an infection that travelled to his joints. I couldn't face another trip to the vet, but Luke had read about a study where a cat with gangrenous mastitis had been treated with a selection of honey, antibiotics and nothing across the sores. Apparently, where the honey was used the sores healed the quickest. The study went on to explain that honey was one of the quickest healing remedies in existence but not much research had been done on it because that didn't pay the bills for the big pharmaceutical companies. So, I began poulticing Pan's leg daily with honey, and after a couple of days the swelling ruptured as the infection was drawn out, and a week later the wound was smaller than a pin prick. As well as this Luke found it helped with his hay fever, and I'd taken to using it instead of sugar, so we were getting through our fair share.

However, I didn't know the first thing about keeping bees, and so Luke arranged for Jack to be my mentor. Jack owned five hives, and it was decided that my hives would be kept at his place until we found a place of our own. With that decided, next Luke found beehives for sale online and so he reached out. He arranged for us to purchase two hives, one complete with swarm, for a second swarm had been promised by El Mexicano's son.

The day we went to see the bees Jack came along too, as an advisor, and we met the beekeeper in the town of Cabrales, where he'd finished up his cafe con leche, chucked a toothpick in his mouth (an accessory that stayed for the duration of our visit) and then motioned for us to follow him in his car. We followed him up to a beautiful pueblo in the mountains and there he swapped his car for a quad bike and motioned for us to get on. We looked at him a little confused, it was a big quad bike but it still didn't look like four people could ride it. He then pointed out exactly where we were to put each of our bums. I took the comfy seat behind the driver, and Luke and Jack hung precariously off the rack on the back.

Once settled the beekeeper climbed into the driving seat and we were off, manoeuvring the tiny pueblo roads much easier in our now downsized vehicle. We came to the edge of the pueblo and the mountains stretched out ahead of us for as far as the eye could see, the sky a perfect shade of blue looking down on a patchwork of purple heather and lush green. It was all common land, the beekeeper explained, and his hives were sprinkled everywhere. We pulled up alongside a collection of hives and as the beekeeper began to fill his smoker with grass, he suggested we put our bee suits on. Neither Luke nor I had one, and on top of that I'd dressed completely inappropriately for the activity, shorts and a T-shirt, having considered the weather and not the activity. Fortunately, Jack had brought a spare beekeeper's suit which I popped on, while Luke took a seat a little way away from the hives. My outfit was finished off with a set of raw hide gloves, and I was dripping within seconds of putting it all on. The beekeeper skipped the gloves, which I thought was rather daring of him, and began transferring two of the swarms that he'd captured the previous week, from the nucleus boxes they were currently in, into proper hives so that they would have time to start filling their frames with honey ready for the winter. One of the swarms was to be mine, and my job was to inspect them and choose the best one.

He directed us to stand behind, out of the bees' flyway and then he began to pump the smoker over the hive, at the same time as he delicately lifted the lid off. Beneath the lid a mass of perfect little bodies writhed, all focussed on their job, seemingly unperturbed by the sudden exposure; the smoke doing its job of keeping the bees calm. With the utmost care the beekeeper began to lift the frames from the nucleus, his bare fingers locating empty corners, and transferred the frames into the brood box of the new hive he had set up beside. Before placing the frame, he gave each a quick check; pointing out the brand-new eggs that had been laid that very morning in the hexagons, showing us the capped hexagons which had been filled with honey, and then in the second box the beekeeper pointed out the Queen. She was much longer than the others and her abdomen was pointed, making her quite easy to distinguish from the smaller, stouter worker bee or the bulky, blunt bottomed drone.

Once both swarms were comfortably settled into their new accommodation we made our way back to the beekeeper's house, and there he insisted we share one of his homemade sidras whilst I decided which hive I wanted. I went for the second, after all, I had met the Queen. The beekeeper pulled out his phone to show us how he'd come to acquire my swarm. He explained how he'd been called to collect it from the roof of a derelict old house that was now being renovated. The film showed hundreds of thousands of bees marching their way into the nucleus, their Queen already in there. Then the camera had panned to the beekeeper. There he stood with his green boiler suit unzipped, no hat, no gloves and a toothpick nonchalantly hanging from his mouth. I asked him in my very broken Spanish how he wasn't getting stung? With a wicked grin he replied that the toothpick stopped them from stinging him.

To complete my second hive, El Mexicano's son offered to call us when one of his beehive's swarmed at his father's finca. And so, we'd been on standby waiting for the call. The first time he'd called us we'd been in town having a coffee, and the combination of goings on and the fact that we were still very much learning Spanish, we just assumed he had a swarm for us. So, we rushed home, threw on long trousers and long shirts, (we were yet to purchase proper suits), and drove ourselves quickly to his farm, only to be met by his whole family and a table laid for lunch. It was his birthday and we'd been invited to the party. Luckily nobody questioned our winter clothes on such a lovely summers day.

The second time he'd called, Luke was sure to repeat the word 'enjambre' numerous times – which means swarm – and this time there was no mistaking it. Once confirmed, knowing that time was of the essence, we raced over to El Mexicano's and Luke jumped out with the hive and begun the arduous journey up the 1-kilometre trail, through the forest and scrub, while I found somewhere to park the car. When I caught up with him, he was a sweaty mess and we dared not think about how we were going to make it back down later that night with a box filled with bees.

Thankfully El Mexicano was already there, preparing to capture the swarm. The bees were carpeting one of the fence posts of the goat pen, where they'd been since the morning and considering it was now 5 p.m., it was highly likely that they wouldn't be hanging around for much longer. El Mexicano directed us as to what to do; Luke collected grass for the smoker, and I was tasked with levelling the hive below the swarm. When he was happy that everything was ready, he lifted the lid off the box and began to lift great handfuls of bees from the post into the box while Luke blew smoke over the swarm. El Mexicano began at the middle of the swarm, where the Queen was most likely to be, and it started promisingly, the bees wandering along the box as I had seen in the beekeeper's video. But then the mood changed, and the bees began to lift off, thickening the air around us.

El Mexicano took over the smoking, trying to guide those bees that were still on the post into the hive. It took quite a time for the bees to settle, but when they had it was impossible to tell if they'd left entirely or if they'd gone into the hive. We were told to come back at 10 p.m., when the sun had set, for the bees would have hopefully settled in the hive and would then be ready for the move.

The return up the dirt track later that evening seemed longer in the gathering dark. More roots to trip over than there'd been in the light. Luke blocked the entrance of the hive with sponge and tape, so that the bees wouldn't be able to leave until we'd settled them at their new home. Then Luke carried the box, while I slowly led him down.

Stag beetles blundered past us, jousting amongst the trees, and Nightjars churred. It was incredible how thick the scrub had grown considering El Mexicano had burnt it only a couple of months earlier. We'd been gutted when we'd turned up to find the side of the hill scorched, finding the charred remains of some sort of ground nesting bird's nest.

Remarkably, given the unevenness of the route, the hive had made it in one piece. We secured the box in the boot and once we were at home, we left the hive in the car with all the windows and the boot thrown open, just in case the bees escaped. An angry swarm in a sealed car was not worth the risk.

Pre-dawn the next day we headed over to Jack's, slightly disconcerted by the fact that we could hear the frames rattling away, something we hadn't heard from the hive we'd brought back from the beekeepers. Jack met us at the entrance to his farm and he confirmed our fear. The hive was empty. For future reference, Jack told us to give the box a slap and the hive would vibrate if there were bees in there. Just to be sure I did it then and it was silent. I took the lid off and there was nothing, maybe twenty or so bees left behind. But the Queen and the rest were gone.

We set the empty hive up beside Jack's hórreo, a spot where he'd had a surprising amount of luck catching swarms before and left.

Chapter 10

The Den

Towards the end of the summer Jack called to say we'd caught ourselves a swarm, and he invited us around to have a look. The bees were busy when we arrived, and I wondered how we would move this hive when the time came. It was balanced on the wooden plank that ran the circuit of the base of the traditional wooden granary, whilst we stood awkwardly to the side on a small stone wall. But Jack wasn't fazed, this was now the third swarm he'd caught at this spot. The first completely by chance after he'd left it there by accident, en route to putting it away and forgetting about it, only to return and find it buzzing. Next, we headed to catch up with our other beehive. Their flight path was also busy with bees coming to and fro from their foraging, and we took a seat to watch them.

Luke spied a Spotted Flycatcher at the top of a chestnut that stood off to our left. It was dipping and diving for something, and then we realised, almost in unison that he was catching my bees.

It was a bit of an odd feeling, watching this beautiful bird stealing my bees. I felt slightly torn, but only for a second, for my bees could well be the difference between this bird making it to its overwintering grounds in sub-Saharan Africa, or not.

On the way home that afternoon Pablo called with a den site for us to film. Pablo had previously explained that the easiest time to observe wolves was when they were denning, for they'd naturally spend a lot of time with the pups. This behaviour also meant it was possible to give ten days' notice in anticipation of filming them, thus fulfilling our permit conditions. The den, Pablo explained, was only 200m off the road, and very close to a village, just on the outskirts of Riaño. Apparently, every day in the late afternoon, the cubs were coming out of the den to play in an open grassy area below their den.

Before filming, we decided to recce the site first. We arrived at 4 p.m. on a Friday evening and parked up around the corner just past a herd of grazing cattle, all seemingly unaware of the wolf den located above them. Pablo dropped a pin for where we should sit, up the valley, on the opposite side of the road to the den. From our view point we could no longer see the road below, but we could clearly see the den and the two open areas. One large and circular, one long and thin like a finger, both where the cubs had been seen playing according to Pablo.

At quarter past seven a rustling in the bushes behind us made my heart pound. I wasn't worried about it being a wolf, I was more worried about it being a Wild Boar which are said to be the most dangerous animal in Europe. They are probably the most persecuted animal in Europe too, which goes some way to explaining their top spot rating as the most dangerous with most injuries by boar being reported by hunters. Once, when we were camping during our project looking for the Iberian Lynx, Luke and I heard something snuffling outside our tent. I assumed it was the campsite's dog, so clapped very loudly to scare it off. With a snort the creature fled, taking out all the tent's guy lines in the process. In the moment it felt like the boar had charged us. Had we not been inside weighting it down, I believe the Wild Boar would have gained a tent that evening. Even knowing that it didn't mean us any harm, it gave me quite a shock and I was still incredibly wary of Wild Boar. Now being sat in a thicket of bushes, with what we thought was a Wild Boar metres from us, I was frozen with fear.

It was an incredibly hot day and I'd taken my shoes and socks off, so I was not at all prepared for a confrontation with a Wild Boar. But then we heard voices. We immediately assumed they were hunters, and my fear grew. There were countless stories of local hunters mistaking people for game. Just a few years before, in a village a couple over from ours, hunters accidentally shot and killed an old lady who'd been hanging her laundry. So, from my perspective, easily more dangerous than a Wild Boar.

Luke stood up to look whilst I hurriedly put my shoes and socks back on, just as two people crashed through the bushes that separated us from the track. They seemed as surprised to see us as we were to see them. We had no wolf luck that first evening, probably not helped by the late arrivals, whose timing coincided with the time Pablo stated the wolves were usually active.

The night was spent in a local pension in Boca de Huergano, and we slept well on a hearty Menu del Dia; a heavy three course meal of mountain food, all for the princely sum of ten euros a head. This set us up perfectly to be in place by 7 a.m. the next morning. It was still dark when we arrived, the first few streaks of blue just starting to appear across the skies. There was fresh wolf scat in the middle of the road en route to our viewing spot, which filled us with hope that we would get lucky this time. Another group of wildlife watchers arrived at half past seven, but continued up the track behind us, and our friends from the day before arrived at ten to eight, just as the sun was rising.

Our mate was the first to spot a wolf, and he kindly talked us through where he'd seen it. All disturbances from the evening before were quickly forgotten as we became a team in our mission to spot the wolf.

Luke was the next to get lucky, as two little grey forms scampered quickly across the bottom of one of the grassy open areas. But as quickly as they appeared they disappeared, and I missed them. Twenty minutes later a wolf appeared in the top corner of the grassy plain, and then a second, and while the first melted into the forest, the second lingered a little while longer. Pacing back and forth a couple of times, sniffing the ground and then the air. They were much smaller than the ones we'd seen with Pablo. This year's pups or maybe yearlings, we guessed.

But they were equally as beautiful, sleek silver-grey coats that blended in perfectly with the drying grass and disappeared instantly at the edge of the forest.

And then a young pup appeared from another corner of the field carrying what looked like a bone. It was so big for the pup that it tripped over the bone a few times before abandoning it and taking interest in something else in the small ditch that ran the length of the field. Diving in, only its waggy tail visible as it dug for whatever it was that'd caught its attention. We watched it for about five minutes and then it too disappeared into the forest that surrounded the circular meadow. Another five or so minutes passed, and our first adult wolf appeared in the same spot as the pup, and it followed a similar route to the pup, allowing us a good view of her slightly darker form. The wolves would appear and disappear from all over the place, making it impossible to get an accurate count on how many there actually were. A second pup appeared on a different rocky outcrop to where the den was, a little lower down, carrying something round and dark in its mouth. It was definitely a different pup to the one that was carrying the bone, so the most certain we could be was that there were at least two pups.

By 11 a.m. the activity was finished. No doubt there was a pile of wolves snoozing somewhere in the forest opposite. When it was clear there was no more to be seen for now, we left, exhilarated by our wonderful wolf-filled morning.

We returned home to a message from Pablo, a press release that stated: 'Councillor Pablo Carlos Suárez-Quiñones Fernández, had ordered the suspension of the hunting of wolves in Castilla y León.' It gave us hope that the wolf pack we'd just been watching were safe for now.

The ban statement went on to read that 'the quota of 143 wolves predicted to be killed by hunters during the present season 2018–2019 was cancelled. And that hunting of wolves in Castilla y León would now be an illegal act, punishable in this season 2018–2019. We invite you to collaborate with the relevant authorities (Guardia Civil – Seprona) to denounce any act of wolf hunting if you are aware of such acts' (a translation of the statement).

The statement also declared that between the years 2016–2019, the administration had authorised the killing of 429 wolves by hunters. A point at the end of the statement did leave room for some concern, for it read that 'however, the Junta de Castilla y León (the local government) does not seem to want to cease its efforts to kill wolves'. The ban was a step forward, but with the local government against the ban, I was worried that we could be about to witness an increase in illegal wolf killings.

Nevertheless, directed by Pablo, and buoyed by Castilla y León's move to stop wolf hunting for the upcoming year, we'd shown our hand and asked outright for permits to set up a hide at the exact location of the wolves' den.

Amazingly the permits were granted, and so to make sure the permission was airtight, Pablo put us in touch with the ranger who was responsible for the area to let him know of our permits and plans.

Chapter 11

A Meeting with the Mayor

Unfortunately, we were not able to take immediate advantage of our access, for we were on a press trip in Estonia, and during the week we were away news about the site spread like wildfire. The weekend before we were set to go film, a nature guide was fined €2,000 for standing in the very field where we'd seen the cubs playing and howling to attract them so that his guests might get a closer look. The park rangers, the locals and the legitimate tour operators were furious. We hoped that the incident would have put off people from visiting, but this was not to be the case.

The day arrived and, armed with government permits and messages of endorsement from the on-duty park ranger, we arrived to find our planned parking space full with four other cars, clearly all there for the wolves. We drove past them for five minutes further up the road, to get Luke sorted and then return once they'd gone. Luke had spotted an entrance to the forest from the road, and if he'd everything ready to go, all it required from me was pulling up and turfing him out. Hopefully the whole drop off would be quick, and no one would be any the wiser of his arrival.

At the lay-by I organised the packed meals I'd made that would last Luke the next three days: a tonne of water, peanut butter sandwiches for breakfast, bananas for lunch, chocolate, digestive biscuits, cakes for snacks, and three Tupperware containers of pasta, risotto and bean salad for dinners. Perhaps a little overkill, but he wasn't going to starve on my watch. Meanwhile Luke was organising his tripod, camera bag and hide, which the night before he'd rubbed down with goat poo in an attempt to mask his human smell and the banquet I'd prepared for him. It is universally agreed by wolf scientists that a wolf's sense of smell is the most acute of all its senses. The hide, and the fact Luke hadn't showered for two days prior, left the car smelling a bit fruity. I dreaded to think what the return would be like.

After a quick bite to eat, we headed back on ourselves. Two cars still remained, the first was a local tour company's but there was no sign of the group, the second was in the process of being packed up by a man who gave us a dirty look as we passed.

'It's now or never,' said Luke. 'I've got to get everything set up before the wolves start getting active, otherwise it will be a complete waste of time.' And so when we came to the spot, I pulled over, Luke jumped out, grabbed his gear from the seat behind and was already off down the side of the bank before I'd pulled away.

I went to grab my phone to put on the chair beside me, just in case he called, only to find Luke's phone still in his seat. Surely, he would realise quickly, otherwise this could be a bit of a problem! I turned the car around, headed back, and sure enough he was now running back up the bank (his gear dumped at the edge of the tree line). Needless to say, it wasn't the smooth drop off we'd planned. But no cars passed during the time, and so I was feeling confident that we hadn't been seen.

I drove to the nearby village and pulled up, waiting to get the go ahead from Luke that he was comfortably set up and that I could go to the hotel and get myself checked in. While Luke was hide bound for the next three days and nights, I'd pulled the long straw and was staying at the same little place as before. Comfortable clean bed and a Menu del Dia each evening was the plan for me. About half an hour later I got a picture from Luke of a pile of sheep's wool on the ground, and a message that read, 'positioned myself on top of this.' A second photo pinged on my phone; a sweaty topless Luke laid on top of bits of sheep wool. Well, at least it would help disguise his human smell I suppose.

When I got to the hotel, I took a nap. Neither of us had slept well the night before and on top of that I think the drive, and the stress of the set-up, had taken its toll. Luke was also settling in for a snooze, so we planned to reconnect in an hour and a half. But just as I was settling down, my phone started buzzing. There was a problem. An old boy, who claimed to be the mayor of the local village, turned up saying that Luke didn't have permission from the pueblo and that the farmers were fed up. He didn't care that Luke had permits, that the land was part of the National Park, he said that this was all irrelevant, for Luke didn't have permission from the farmers. The people that mattered.

Luke negotiated with the mayor, and after a few more words, the mayor had backtracked a little, saying he personally didn't have a problem with Luke, but the local tour companies did. He was actually there on their behalf, not the farmers'. Apparently, the local wild watching guiding company, the one whose car we'd seen parked up, the one we hoped hadn't seen Luke running back and forth to the tree line, had seen us after all. And they had been the one to call us in.

The mayor continued, for while they were on the subject, he wasn't particularly happy with the tour operators either. The sheep wool Luke was set up on had been dumped there the week before by one of the wildlife guides, a move to bait the wolves. At that point it had been a full carcass, so clearly someone had made a good meal of it. And that was what the mayor was most angry about. That someone had put a carcass out for the wolves, which could teach them to eat sheep, he said. He was angry about how much money these wildlife watchers and photographers had, whilst farmers had no money. That they were the ones who were expected to live with the wolves eating their animals. He showed Luke videos of wolf-savaged cows, to enforce his point. The wolves had killed a young horse only the week before, and seven calves in total last year. He spoke about how the hunters were better than the wildlife watchers, for at least they paid his village to shoot a Roe Deer. Meanwhile, his village got no money when a Roe Deer was killed by a wolf. 'The wolves don't bring any money, they just take money,' he said.

After venting his anger at the wolves and the photographers, the mayor left Luke with his number in case there were any further issues. Somehow, even though Luke was one of the photographers being grumbled about, Luke won the mayor over and was given his blessing to stay.

We could both completely understand the frustration of the locals. Surely the tour companies should be working with them directly on this. Increasing tourism to see the wolf had to benefit those who were affected by them. If it didn't, well then tourism had no chance of helping the wolf's case. If anything, it would only make it harder. Luke had set up camp in the middle of a storm. And on top of all that, he'd been found topless with only a pair of camouflage long johns on, taking a nap. What a sight he must have been; a skinny, half-naked English boy camped in the middle of a known wolf den.

Chapter 12

The Way of Wildlife

The next morning, I was up at six, ready to get myself in position on the opposite side of the valley to Luke and his hide, in the same place we'd sat the last time to watch the wolves. It was minus two degrees Celsius when I got in the car and with no word from Luke during the night, I couldn't stop my mind from horrible thoughts of hypothermia. It took twenty minutes driving through darkness from my hotel to the site. Fresh dung covered the road, and I came around one turning to be faced with a herd of twenty or so of the giant local work horses. They spooked at the car's lights, jumping in fright out of the road and into the bushes as I slowly made my way through them. A little further along another dung shape suddenly revealed eyes, and I brought the car to a stop once again as a Nightjar lifted off from the tarmac. At seven I pulled over in the village closest to the wolf den. There was still no reply from Luke to my message, 'did you survive? Please have messaged me by the time I have got there.' So, I called. He didn't pick up, but to my relief he messaged immediately. 'I'm awake but it's dark. Can't talk. Very uncomfortable. Not cold, actually quite cosy!' 'Any wolf howls last night?' I asked. 'No, but some other weird noises. Owl. Lots of Red Deer.'

There was already a car, a camper and a minivan at the parking spot by the time I arrived. All the vehicles' occupants had already made their way to the viewing spots, and by the time I made it up to mine, people were already settled there. I managed to find a spot just to the left of them.

As the sun rose a little higher, I could see that I'd found myself an even better spot than before. There was only space for one bottom, which was probably why it was still free, but I was now sat a little higher with a completely clear view of the opposite side of the valley. Four minutes after arriving, excited whispers started and sure enough a wolf had appeared in the open. I couldn't see Luke, but I guessed it stood just to the left of where he was positioned and messaged him saying so. And then two more wolves appeared in the middle of the open space, a mother and cub. Surely right in front of Luke. They greeted each other playfully, licked and nuzzled, and then the mother led them both into the tree line and out of sight. 'You are not going to believe this,' wrote Luke. 'They did all that playing behind a damn bush.' But that is the way of wildlife, of course.

Another larger wolf appeared to Luke's right, but he didn't hang around long. And that was the extent of our wolf sightings that morning, all in the space of about fifteen minutes. The sightings hadn't been short, but neither had they allowed for much filming or photography. Getting good natural history footage of the Iberian Wolf was not going to be easy. But at least none of the wolves had given the slightest bit of notice to Luke's presence.

At nine thirty (only an hour after our last wolf sighting) the minibus group, who had been sitting further up the hill behind me, had clearly decided that that was it from the wolves for the day, and were now making their way, very loudly, back down. Fourteen passed on the track behind me: English, Irish, Spanish and German, and they were chatting away so loudly that had the wolves had any intentions of returning, I was pretty sure they would probably think better of it.

For me it was back to the hotel for a nap, for Luke it was a second day trying to get comfortable in the now 32 degrees heat. A little later that evening Luke messaged. A man had just turned up, crashing through the undergrowth, and had set up a hide metres from Luke. Luke had messaged the ranger, who confirmed that they didn't have permission but there was nothing he could really do about it. It was very frustrating. No wolves that evening, and the guy had left just after dark, only to return the next morning to once again set his hide up directly next to Luke. It turned out that the man was English. A couple of days previously he had been part of the tourist group that had reported Luke, and then had returned alone because 'he couldn't resist'. He had no idea you needed permits, and he clearly had no understanding of wildlife.

Meanwhile, I was up the hill and had been the first to arrive. My neighbours from the day before turned up about 20 minutes later and they clearly hadn't realised I was sat the other side of the rock from them. I should have made my presence known immediately but I wasn't anticipating one of the pair to choose his poo-ing spot but five metres behind me. What made matters worse was that he was clearly suffering from a dodgy stomach, and I was privy to every splatter. I coughed loudly and finally, after the third time he retreated in fright. Between the crappy field craft and the dicky tummy, the wolves had steered well clear.

Chapter 13

Offer Accepted

With the summer ending, wolf pups now joining their packs and spending less and less time at the den, the opportunity to film them passed. And coming up next, we had a long stint of travel for work planned, two months working with tourist boards and local tour operators in Ecuador, Australia, Zambia and Malawi. The goats and chooks were being looked after by some friends. We had also made a decision. Having made various offers on Wild Finca (our first being a very insulting price El Mexicano had suggested), we were finally going back to offer a figure right on the very edge of our budget.

We must have seen perhaps twenty or so more properties. Luke more than that even, for I had given up due to the property agents constantly ignoring our budget and showing us spots for more than double what we could afford. I'm sure they'll take an offer, the agents had said. Surely not a third of what they are asking, I had replied. But even after all that, nowhere else held a candle to Wild Finca. Land too steep, too much wood, too little meadow, too far from civilisation, too much eucalyptus. Even the ones that were perfect on paper just didn't have 'the feeling'.

There was only one other property which we seriously considered. A beautiful old mill tucked away at the bottom of a valley, a river running through it, surrounded by lush wildflower meadows. We first saw it in spring, and it was breathtaking. The tranquil sound of running water, and the swathes of wildflowers, it had captivated us. But the agent (quite un-agent-like) suggested we spoke to a Dutchman, who knew a lot about the property, before making any decisions. The Dutchman was good friends with the previous owners, and he'd spent a lot of time there helping with renovations. We'd visited the Dutchman at his home for a cup of tea, and during our meeting he'd talked us out of buying the old mill. You see, we'd only ever visited the mill during the spring, perhaps the most gracious months for viewing any home: good lighting, a warm breeze, the apple trees in blossom, it had looked a romantic prospect. But the reality was that for much of the year the mill sat in a thick fog which rose from the stream. Then when the rains came it flooded and remained so for months. Without the Dutchman there would likely have been no Wild Finca, and we would have instead been sat in a waterlogged old mill, battling endless damp.

And so, on the last day of September, we'd returned to Wild Finca to make our final offer.

When the BFG accepted our offer, it was a very emotional moment. I felt quite overwhelmed and gave him a big hug, which took him by surprise. He was a man of little words, but he told us that he'd lived there since he was sixteen years old. And, given that he was now somewhere in his late seventies, Wild Finca was the only home he could remember. 'This farm is in my blood,' he told us. He didn't have any children, but he'd always hoped that his nephew might take on the property. However, like so many of the younger generation from these mountain communities, the nephew instead had chosen to move to the city.

Fortunately, the property was only to be split between the BFG, a sister, and the two children of a deceased brother. A dream case our solicitor called it, who at the same time had been working on a purchase where the sellers had one hundred and three claimants.

The purchase went as smoothly as we'd anticipated and, on the day we completed, we headed straight to our new home from the city. Under a brilliant blue sky, we sat at a spot we'd named the mound, surveying our new kingdom, drinking in our exceptional fortune. And then a man pulled up to the top of our drive. He jumped out and started talking into a walkie talkie. Not long after that, the cries of hunting dogs could be heard, yelping and yowling from the forest below, and three men in high-vis jackets appeared at the top of Wild Finca's boundary. Without a second thought, they'd strode out into the thick of our new fields, sending their dogs out to clear any animal that dared seek shelter. There was nothing we could do. We felt angry, and as much as we wanted to kick them off then and there, we managed to talk each other down. After all, it was likely they had no idea the farm had been sold, and we imagined that the BFG must have allowed them to hunt the land. We hoped it would just be a matter of letting them know it was no longer huntable. Though I had conflicting feelings about hunting, it was a hard no on our land. Wild Finca was intended to be a haven. Moreover, we had just discovered that we would soon welcome our very own wild creature into the world—I was expecting our first child.

Part 2

Establishing Roots

Chapter 14

Where to Start

Of course, Wild Finca wasn't called Wild Finca when we bought it, it was a name we came up with as we felt it reflected our intentions for our home: to turn it into a wild farm. When we bought Wild Finca we agreed that we would rewild the majority of it. A concept we'd first come across after filming at the pioneering rewilding project, Knepp. Twenty years ago, Knepp stopped intensively farming their 3,500-acre estate, and instead allowed nature to take the driver's seat. The sheer abundance of nature that returned was astonishing, with endangered species such as Turtle Doves, Nightingales and Purple Emperor Butterflies finding sanctuary there. We were so inspired by what they'd done, we dreamed of doing something similar ourselves one day. Now that we had Wild Finca, we actually could. And so, we planned to restore the land to its natural, uncultivated state. Taking a hands-off approach and allowing the landscape to do exactly as it wished. However, there were a few exceptions, a few plots that we'd chosen for ourselves to exist within. And so, after returning from our travels it was these that we got started with. One of which was the food forest.

The day the Dutchman talked us out of buying the old mill, aside from giving us invaluable property advice, he'd also shown us around his home, which included his pride and joy, a food forest. Made up of all types of fruiting trees and bushes that directly or indirectly benefit humans, a food forest is planted in a way designed to mimic that of a natural forest ecosystem. Producing food efficiently and sustainably, as well as boosting biodiversity. It was our first encounter with a food forest, and it had been a bit of a light-bulb moment.

With winter now truly upon us, whilst it wasn't a great time to start any building work, it was the perfect time for tree planting. The plot we chose for the food forest lay at the bottom of our driveway. It was easy to access, got good sunlight and was relatively flat. The first tree we planted was an apple tree, a type called a Roxelia. To most it seemed an odd choice, for we were surrounded by apple trees, we even had an old orchard full of them. But they were all sidra making apples, not good for eating, whereas the Roxelia was. This was followed by a series of berry bushes and eighteen more fruit trees. More eating apple varieties, plum, persimmon, apricot, nectarine, cherry and pear. But a few weeks later a deluge of rain washed away many of the saplings, and we'd found them scattered around the plot. After replanting, and with no further torrents of rain that season, most of the trees survived their baptism to Asturian winters.

We also found ourselves bending the originally agreed rules of 'taking a hands-off approach and allowing the landscape to do exactly as it wished', as we began cutting willow whips and replanting them along the fence line in the hope that they would grow into a living fence. Furthermore, we'd agreed for a local farmer to continue the grazing of the land for the time being, for we realised that if we really did leave it to its own devices it would eventually all turn to forest, and we didn't want that. We liked the mosaic we currently had, it could certainly do with a few more hedges, connectivity for wildlife, perhaps more diversity in the plant species and not just the coveted grass for grazers. But what we didn't want was Wild Finca to become one large block of woodland. We appreciated that this didn't exactly fit with the original definition of rewilding that we knew of, and so we decided that more exploration of the idea would be required. Each time we visited Wild Finca we'd take Pan and Coco, who would frolic manically as we worked, and then would curl up asleep in the back of the Skidonk while we stopped for coffee with our neighbour Olaya. Olaya was El

Mexicano's distant cousin and at our first meeting she'd insisted we always stop by for a coffee. Despite the fact Olaya didn't drink coffee, ('horrible stuff', she'd told us) yet somehow, she'd learnt to make a very nice cup of it, nevertheless. She'd make us sit at the small table in her kitchen, on the only two chairs in the room, while she bustled around cleaning glasses and preparing the cafetière. Olaya was tiny and when she was standing, she was as tall as we were when sitting down. But she could be ferocious in the way she talked about others, particularly in the village, and Luke and I made a rule to make sure we never got on the wrong side of her.

Olaya had lived in her house for fifty years and we knew we could learn a lot from her about our new home. It was on Olaya's advice that we moved our beehives on 1 March. The first day of spring, the day her mother had always done it. We placed them on the boundary line of the food forest, facing down the valley. It was a spot that got sun all day, and it was also in prime position for them to pollinate our food forest. It seemed like the perfect location for them until a late storm hit and we turned up the next day to find the beehives strewn across the food forest floor. What we didn't know when placing them was that when the high winds arrived, the valley acted like a funnel whipping the gusts into a frenzy that would crescendo on our land. The hives took quite a battering but remarkably the bees survived it, and we'd stacked them back up and crossed our fingers. The practice is that if you move a beehive you need to move it at least two miles away, otherwise the bees keep returning to their old hive. This meant that we would be unable to move them within Wild Finca. If it didn't work out again at that location then we'd probably have to move them back to Jack's for a time, before relocating them elsewhere on our land.

Shortly after the bees moved in, some more tenants joined Wild Finca. Four of Isabel and Angel's (our old landlord's) sheep, advertised as a housewarming gift, but really, we were doing them a favour for their sheep flock was forever escaping due to a lack of grazing. Whilst it had previously only been our vegetable patch that suffered, more recently the sheep had turned their attention to the beautifully tended front garden at Casa Angel. They'd stripped the grapevines, and not a single rose survived their rampaging. And so, Angel had reluctantly agreed to Isabel's request to downsize their flock, and two females, and two lambs were moved across in the back of the Skidonk one afternoon. They'd not quite known what to do with all the grass and had stood frozen for some time before tentatively taking a step forward into the green. We'd have liked to have moved the goats over at the same time, for they were probably partly responsible for the disappearance of both grapevine and rose, and they'd also taken to escaping onto the roof of Angel's workshop behind the rental, but the current fencing situation at Wild Finca was useless, as it had been erected for the BFG's cattle herd, and Pan and Coco would weave in and out of it on our walks of the land, proving its ineffectiveness. While the sheep would unlikely move from the field they were put in, kept there by ample grazing, the goats were far too nosy and so couldn't be trusted to stay in one place. So, until we moved over, they would have to stay with us at the rental.

As the days began to grow longer and warmer, and the first Egyptian Vulture arrived, we'd turned our minds to where we were going to live. An old camper van, plonked at any spot on the land, would have suited us nicely. That is, had it just been the two of us. However, with a little one on the way, we agreed that something more substantial was necessary. But where to start took a bit more figuring out. Surely, we could quickly convert the hórreo where the BFG had been living. Replacing the scrunched-up animal feedbags in the wall holes with glass would be an easy upgrade, bringing in light and warmth. However, the roof was just tiles with no insulation, so that would need redoing as well. The upstairs was truly tiny, with just enough room for a bed. In a small, boxed-off corner, there was a fireplace that had been used by the old man to smoke his meat, leaving the walls blackened from years of chorizo making. As for the downstairs, the floor was dirt and rock, piled high with all manner of rubbish, including a stack of old magazines from the top shelf at the shops. All in all, converting the hórreo might be a bigger job than we initially thought. We also considered converting the two small grain stores into a mini house; upstairs and downstairs connected by a spiral staircase to save space. Undoubtedly cool, but not particularly practical with a baby. The farmhouse was far too big a job, both physically (there was no chance it would be ready in time for baby's arrival) and financially. The old barn, which was more walnut tree than building, was the frontrunner for a while. We even went so far as to draw up plans for it: an open-plan kitchen, living room and bathroom downstairs, and a mezzanine bedroom upstairs. But planning permission was hard to come by and although everyone told us to just go for it without, after all everyone else did, the work would have been obvious, and we didn't know our neighbours well enough to be sure they wouldn't denounce us (report us to the local authorities). For it wasn't just our neighbours we were concerned about reporting us. There was a public footpath that snaked its way through Wild Finca, dividing our land for the most part in two. It allowed walkers a bird's-eye view of whatever it was we were up to.

That left us with one final option, to convert the hay loft of the cow barn. I hadn't seen its potential for a long time, the only access was up a rickety ladder, and the space was packed to the rafters with rotting hay and rats' nests, so it had been very hard to visualise what could be done with it. But Luke saw what it could be turned into. It took Luke a week of clearing it out, trying to get rid of the overwhelming smell of rodent piss, before I could be convinced. We asked a friend, who in a previous life had managed huge building sites across the

US, to come over and confirm that it was structurally sound enough to hold what we'd planned for the conversion. A two-bedroom, two-bathroom, open plan kitchen and living room. He popped over one afternoon, walked around the building twice outside, and then twice inside, before telling us that the building was completely unstable and could very possibly fall down tomorrow. My face dropped. Camper van it was then. Before he'd burst into peals of laughter and told us that he was joking and that it was structurally sound and would withstand whatever we wanted to throw at it. I am sure there are more technical ways of checking these things, but his words were good enough for us. Next, it was time to find a team of builders to do the work.

Luke was desperate to get stuck in himself, however, before realising we were expecting a baby, we'd Crowdfunded a documentary to tell the story of the Nightingale. Enthralled by the magic of bird migration, we wanted to make a film that shared this remarkable phenomenon in an engaging and exciting way. A film that not only appealed to bird-lovers but all sorts of folk, with all different interests. We realised that as a character the epochal Nightingale could do just that, engage with a variety of audiences, whilst being the poster species for telling the stories of all our migratory birds. And so, with Luke travelling for shoots, I was left in charge of overseeing the work.

Chapter 15

A Baby Boy

Via Jack we'd met Ali, a lovely lady who with her husband and two young girls had been living in the area for five years. She'd invited me to hers to make soap, and during that time she'd mentioned an English builder who she knew. I'd taken the number, said builder had visited, and from there he gave us a quote to put a team together that could realise our vision. The price fitted our budget and with time against us, the eight to ten weeks he anticipated the job to take would have meant we'd be in with a month to spare before baby joined us. As he'd come recommended, it was more of a case of 'when can you start?'

Two weeks later work on the barn began and, as well as project managing a barn conversion, I was also busy getting on with the job of being pregnant. We'd decided on a home birth. Again, Ali had hooked us up, this time by hosting a lunch and inviting a Spanish midwife who'd trained in the UK and spoke perfect English. My Spanish was limited to wildlife and cooking conversations, so giving birth in a foreign language was too terrifying a prospect for me. In hindsight, I perhaps let our midwife's English skills outweigh some of the other aspects that ultimately proved to be quite important. She was very alternative, not that that is a bad thing, but one of the first things we'd felt the need to clarify was that Luke and I weren't that alternative, despite what many of our friends might think. (Moving to a finca in northern Spain can get you pigeonholed.) But the midwife assured us that wouldn't be a problem, and we had felt placated. After all, wild animals gave birth every day on their own, and we were at our core animals, so why did humans feel the need to complicate such a natural event? How hard could it be?

Builder and midwife in place, I was feeling pretty smug about how smoothly it was all going. Of course, the plain sailing began to hit a few waves soon after. It all started the weekend Luke was home from a shoot, and we'd roped two of his friends into visiting and helping us with some fencing. So far, the sheep had stayed put, and even surprised us with a little lamb. But the goats were becoming bigger liabilities by the day. Pan had got caught upside down in the fence trying to escape to greener grass, and I had nearly gone into labour trying to release him, so they needed moving to Wild Finca as soon as possible. And so, in exchange for sidra and tortilla, Ollie and Michael had come to give us a hand in securing some of the land.

After a long day at Wild Finca we'd headed back to the rental for showers, pre-heading into town for the promised sidra. Just as we were leaving, a tall young chap with waist-length dreadlocks started walking up the driveway towards our rental. He was English and looking for us. Apparently, he was here to work for us, which was the first we'd heard of it. He'd meant to be meeting our main builder, but the young guy's bus arrived late, and the main builder had gone on to a party. So, with no idea of our address, his phone out of battery, he decided to find somewhere to spend the night and remarkably found an empty barn, just on the hill above our rental. Once settled in amongst the hay, he'd lit a spliff and proceeded to get nice and high. It didn't take long before the farmer, whose barn it was, spotted a light and went to investigate. He'd found our new friend, completely spaced out, snuggled in a pile of hay, smoking a joint. On being kicked out our new friend took a last-ditch attempt and asked the farmer if he knew of any young English people, which it just so happened the farmer did, and pointed the guy down to our rental. To this day we don't know which farmer it was, but as the only young English couple we were becoming quite well known in the area.

We dropped the young chap off at Wild Finca, for the crew were sleeping in the old farmhouse, and we'd spent the following weeks keeping an ear out to hear what rumours of us might be going around after the incident. But the raised eyebrows we got as we drove to and from our new home were not new, for while most young people were moving to the cities, which was seen as progressive, us choosing to move to Wild Finca was causing all sorts of confusion.

Aside from his dependence on weed, our new friend turned out to be the hardest worker of the lot. For much of the work I had a spy on the inside who told me so. While Luke was away filming, my parents came out to help me. During the day, while my mum stayed at the rental with me, my dad took on the role of labourer at Wild Finca. From painting to being (as he described it) a one-man chain-gang digging a trench through rock and flint to lay our sewage pipeline (I'd argue that he was the hardest worker of the team). But despite all this, time dragged on, budget kept being exceeded, and the finish date, of a month pre-due date, came and went. Before long, due date was upon us.

The home birth did not go according to plan either. After thirty-four hours labouring at home, including three hours pushing, I finally managed to convince Luke that this clearly wasn't working and to burn the birth plan. And, against my midwife's advice Luke took me to hospital. Conveniently situated just down the road, we'd been at the hospital in under ten minutes, and within half an hour I was being checked over by a doctor. I was seven centimetres dilated, so miles yet from the pushing stage, and the baby's head was at an odd angle. Their recommendation was an emergency c-section. 'Don't do it, you'll regret it,' was the advice of my midwife. But I was already halfway out of the consultancy room, following the doctor to a surgery that wasn't quite ready for me. Luke couldn't be in theatre with me, but our son was delivered healthy and whole (albeit with a bit of a cone-shaped head) at seven in the morning. They lay him against me for a moment and then he'd been whisked away. After being weighed and whatever else it is they do to a newborn, he was given to Luke on the other side of the door, and I saw the pair of them fleetingly before being wheeled to recovery. I lost a lot of blood during the surgery, and so I was kept separate from Luke and baby for the next three hours. For me, in and out of consciousness, knowing that our baby was safe with Luke, it wasn't so bad. But for Luke, who was not kept updated on my progress and had convinced himself they were trying to find the best way to break the news to the English man that the mother hadn't made it, it must have a been a trying time.

When we were finally reunited, I was enthralled; what an astonishing creature a newborn baby is! Their sweet earthy smell, their miniature everything. Utter perfection. We named him Roan after the magnificent Roan antelope of Zambia. A nod to the place Luke and I had first met. And from that moment on, time, direction, motivation, well, everything changed for us.

Chapter 16

Food Forest Fails

We didn't move much from our bed those first weeks, and after that we only moved as far as the wildflower meadow behind the rental. It was a beautiful spot to sit quietly with our new baby, amongst the Tongue Orchids, Yarrow and Quaking Grass, watching endless butterflies dance by. Luke taught Roan what made it such a great wildflower meadow, 'the Yellow Rattle, you see, it's known as the meadow-maker.' And he'd explain to our weeks' old son, who was already showing signs of being a great botanist, how once Yellow Rattle germinated, its roots would seek out the surrounding grass and take its nutrients causing the grass to die, creating more space for wildflowers to thrive. The reason this field was such a showstopper was all thanks to our neighbour, a chap in his late seventies, who tended the plot in the traditional way. He would hand cut it once a year with a scythe, preparing it to feed his animals through the winter months, and he had done so ritually for many years. When moving day finally came, the old boy had gifted us a few bales from that field, so that we could try and mirror that magnificent meadow across the grassy fields at Wild Finca.

And moving day couldn't have come sooner. We'd had a bit of bad luck, losing a chicken and seven chicks the night I'd given birth to Roan. My poor dad having to break the news the day he met his new grandson. The two remaining chicks from the lost brood had taken to roosting on Pan's horns which he didn't think much of, so the move to Wild Finca, with more space and a private goat bedroom couldn't have come soon enough.

The chickens were moved into the two old grain storage buildings, which Luke and my dad had converted into a rather impressive coop by cutting out a door at the bottom and running fencing around the outside to create a protected outdoor area. The goats originally joined the sheep, but Coco went from beating up the chickens to beating up the sheep, so they had to be separated. Unfortunately, the fencing we had put up with Michael and Ollie proved fruitless against the will of Pan and Coco, who were constantly escaping, oftentimes ending up on the staircase, front feet over the barn door, heads peering in the kitchen, trying their hardest to clamber in. And we found ourselves spending more and more time trying to contain them, over getting other jobs around the farm done.

The first time we managed to visit with Olaya, after officially moving in the month before, she had bustled us straight in, and then set about making coffee as usual. Roan was asleep in the carrier on my front and Olaya chattered away as she pottered. I could feel myself going redder and redder as understanding dawned. It may have been our first time stopping by, but she'd already met some of her new neighbours. Just a few days earlier she'd woken from her siesta to find Pan and Coco wandering around her bedroom. They'd let themselves in the front door, which was open that afternoon to give the house a blast of fresh air and made their way along the bungalow corridor and into Olaya's bedroom. Apparently, they were very polite house guests, just the one little poo in the corridor, and to her credit she saw the funny side of the whole event. Olaya had kept animals all her life, so it wasn't a completely novel experience. Beneath the main house still slept a small flock of sheep, a traditional way of heating the building, and Olaya had raised many an orphaned lamb in the kitchen where we were now sat. But we knew how bolshy our goats could be, they'd long been banned from our own house for jumping on the sideboards and we feared their next visit would end in disaster. With visions of her waking up to find them dancing around the kitchen counters, or frolicking on top of her in bed, keeping them firmly enclosed at all times had become a priority.

As we sipped on scalding hot coffee, she on her water, the matter of fencing arose. It was the main reason we'd stopped by in the first place. It wasn't just to keep the goats in, but also to address the hunting situation we'd stumbled across on the day we'd completed our purchase of Wild Finca. We'd managed to get hold of the number of the local hunting association and sent a message explaining how we were now the owners of Wild Finca, and how we would prefer it if they refrained from hunting on our land. The message appeared to be delivered and so we hoped that to be the end of that. But to enforce the matter, we were still keen to start fencing our boundary.

The fence that was in the worst shape, thus making it the most pressing to sort, divided Olaya's land from ours. We'd already hired two Venezuelan chaps to make a start on it. We'd met them as they'd been doing some work for Olaya, but on their first day with her they'd taken a left instead of a right and ended up at ours. One of the men, Carlos, spoke very good English and in that first meeting he'd explained that they were political migrants. In Venezuela, Carlos had worked for a zoo rehabilitating wildlife, and it turned out that we had a few connections from our work in South America. He'd been friendly and interesting, and I'd taken his number that day. Now he and his cousin had returned to do some work for us.

The fencing started just fine, simply following the old fallen fence line, and with the ground soft, the posts went in easily. But then they'd hit a rocky vein, at a spot where our land falls into Olaya's, and the two chaps had come to us saying it was impossible for them to erect anything by hand that would last any great length of time along the same course as the old fence. And so, that was what we'd gone over to discuss with Olaya when she'd casually told us about her visit from our unruly goats.

After coffee we'd walked the unforgiving land to discuss the options, and Olaya agreed that the new fence could go below the fall, where the ground was softer. Hopefully here it would also stop the degradation of our land edge, no doubt sped up by Olaya's tenant farmer's cows and his already obvious tendency to overgraze. As it was one of the main fence lines of ours that bordered land owned by someone else, it was a particularly important one to secure against the goats wandering. It was also one of the borders of our food forest.

However, fencing the goats turned out to be an impossible feat. They were Houdinis who saw our attempts to keep them in one place as outright challenges for them to escape. Once the fencing failed, we also tried staking them on long leashes around the land. But if they didn't become completely tangled, one of them would inevitably escape leaving the other crying loudly at being abandoned. Nothing we did could keep them both in the spot we wanted them to be in for very long. Sooner or later they would end up back at the house, most often on their new favourite place to play, the hórreo roof. They would use the roof of the lean-to garage as a ramp to get up, and once they were up there, there was no getting them down, unless they wanted to. Charging up and down, head butting each other, knocking down tiles. All we could do was watch on helplessly as they missed falling off the roof by inches. Once they were done with their games, or sunbathing (another favourite pastime of Pan's that took place in the same spot), they'd go searching for food. And, as goats are browsing animals, who prefer to eat their meals with their heads raised, they'd taken a particular liking to all the green new trees we were planting.

There were many hurdles to overcome with the food forest that first year, another being our inability to keep on top of the grass and, as a result, we lost a few saplings to their being outcompeted. To try and combat this we bought a pair of Chinese geese; to not only eat the grass and weeds, but we chose this breed as they were known for their sociable temperament. Growing up, my grandparents had kept a pair of very aggressive domestic white geese, particularly the female named Queeny. No one ever volunteered to go and see if she'd laid any eggs. I was slightly concerned about getting geese, but fortunately the pair turned out to be very sweet.

We also bought a selection of duck eggs to hatch ourselves. Indian Runner ducks, the upright fellows that waddle a bit like a Penguin. Aylesbury ducks, chubby little white characters, best known as Jemima Puddle-Duck from the Beatrix Potter stories. And Cayuga ducks, a beautiful iridescent greenish black duck that laid black eggs. They had all hatched and I thought they seemed a reasonable number to be getting on with, and then Luke had returned home from running errands one day with a boot full of Muscovy ducklings, large, heavy-bodied ducks with long necks. (Another day it was a pair of chickens, swapped for a bag of chicken feed. After that I stopped letting Luke run errands alone.)

Nevertheless, both the geese and the ducks fulfilled their roles nicely; and while the geese kept the grass down, the ducks did a good job at controlling the slugs and snails (particularly the runner ducks). Plus, they laid yummy eggs, and their poop acted as free fertiliser.

At the bottom of the driveway we built a pond for them, so that run-off from the fuente at the top of our driveway could be captured. And, within the food forest we built them a shelter where they were locked in at night. Foxes were very active around the area, even if according to Olaya wolves were not. However, Pablo believed otherwise. Not long after our move he dropped by to see Wild Finca and meet Roan, and during his visit he'd told us that a friend of his, a local park ranger, believed that our land was where the territory of two wolf packs crossed over. We'd walked with Pablo to a spot just above the forest, which gave clear views of the open mountain face opposite, and he'd said confidently, 'If you stand right here with a scope for one day, and watch that hill over there, you are going to see a wolf!' We were sceptical, after all, Olaya had lived here nearly sixty years and she'd told us that during that time they'd never been seen in or near our village, and they never would be as they would never cross the river that divided where they were from us. Either way, if they were around, then they were welcome. It was time for us to prove our belief that living alongside wolves was possible. And not just wolves, but all wildlife.

Chapter 17

Making a Home for Wildlife

Amidst the goat wrangling and fencing there was other important work to be done. Like tending the wildflower meadow that sits to the left as you enter Wild Finca. It is beautiful, not quite on par with the one behind our old rental, nevertheless, left to its own devices grass would take over and so to maintain it Luke needed to cut it. His intention was to also elevate its diversity by sprinkling the gifted bales. With Wild Finca we inherited a rack of scythes, the BFG clearly well versed in the old ways of tending the land. However, they clearly hadn't been used in a while for all the scythes needed new handles, the woodworm long since disintegrating the original ones. Once replaced Luke began cutting the field by hand. It was exhausting work, and Luke made slow progress, so I shouldn't have been surprised by what happened next. (I will put it down to a small baby taking up most of my bandwidth that, in fact, it had come as a bit of a shock.) One day, Luke returned with an expensive mechanical contraption called a segadora. It was essentially a heavy-duty, hand-managed hay cutter—a lawn mower on steroids. However, it didn't perform well on our land, and neither did Luke. He struggled within just a few lengths of the field, trying to navigate the uneven and steep slopes with the cumbersome equipment. The segadora managed to cover a generous quarter of the field before giving out. Roan and I watched as Luke lost control down the hill for the third time, but this time, he and the segadora crashed unceremoniously into the fence. It was a miracle they didn't go through the fence and into the driveway. Unsurprisingly, the segadora couldn't be resurrected after that impact. Only a couple of days after bringing it home, he sold it on for a sixth of what he paid for it. It was a painful lesson, but it did make him realise that perhaps jobs such as these were better and more reliably done by hand, as demonstrated by our old neighbour. Plus, this method allowed the butterflies, wasp spiders and praying mantises a chance to escape.

A second job Luke embarked on with gusto was pond building. Wild Finca had no year-round standing water, the only water that remained by the end of the summer was that which had been left in the old bathtubs used as water troughs for the cattle. An ingenious adaptation, apart from for the smaller wildlife which we had been having to save throughout the summer, most sadly dead having gone in search of water and then not being able to get out. But one time we had managed to rescue one of the beautiful bright green Iberian rock lizards. And so, in locations he'd earmarked at our very first visit to Wild Finca, with the help of a digger, a month after moving in, two large ponds had been dug. The first was located a stone's throw from home, beneath a giant pear tree, 'Surely the biggest pear tree in the world,' Luke often observed, for it was rather huge. The second, a stone's throw from the first, further into the field beyond. Both were areas of heavily compacted ground where much of the rainwater from the buildings ran off to. As the ground there was clay the ponds had been left to see if they might hold water as they were.

One morning I'd been surprised to see Angel at the bottom of my stairs. Unfortunately, Luke was out, so I had muddled through with much huffing and eye-rolling from Angel. Most Asturians I met were very accommodating of my poor Spanish, but not Angel. Olaya was perhaps my other fiercest critic, 'you really don't understand me at all!' she would say. A sentence that I understood quite well, thank you. But whilst Olaya may have been blunt, she was never nasty, at least not to my face. Angel, on the other hand, seemed to get irate every time he found himself having to converse with me. Despite his obvious frustration at me, the way his face would go red, a vein on his forehead would throb, and the way he would talk faster and louder, I thought I'd got the gist of the issue. Angel wanted a sheep back, as one of his had died. Apparently gifting meant something different in Asturias. Or perhaps we'd just misunderstood him. When Angel left, I sent Luke a WhatsApp relaying the message I had taken from the conversation, only for him to reply that Angel had just called, scolded him for having a woman who spoke no Spanish, and then asked for a sheep back as one of his had died. With the surprise lamb it left us where we'd started, so no real loss after all, especially as we were away for the end of summer. I was staying with my parents in France while Luke was away guiding in Brazil, and then when he got back my sister was getting married, one less animal was only a good thing for our house sitters. Having said that, one less sheep didn't make life much easier, one less goat on the other hand might have.

Luckily, our American house sitters were retired farmers and had lots of experience with goats. But our pair put them through their paces. We'd been having some success with electric fencing at this stage with the goats. Small plots, moved frequently, not too far from the farmhouse, and brought into the barn each night made the goats feel sufficiently special enough that they'd been staying put. Or maybe it had been the right sort of grass, who knows. But the system began to fail for the house sitters. They would fix the fence only to turnaround and find the goats had broken out again, and again, and again. In the end the husband had resorted to transforming the old walnut barn into 'the goat palace'. Using old bits of wood from around the place, they'd blocked the gaping entrance with a sturdy fence and a very fine door. The handy husband had also fashioned a sort of playground inside, and the goats loved it. So, they spent most of their time in there with a hay net during our absence.

Things had been going very well after that, that was until the day before my sister's wedding, and four days before we were due home. We received a phone call saying the house sitters couldn't take it anymore and we had to come home immediately. I could only imagine what the goats had done this time. Except, as I translated snippets of what Luke was relaying to me (he had been the one to take the call), it wasn't the goats this time, it was the ducklings. So many dead ducklings, too many for the wife to cope with. A complete bloodbath.

We finally got the full story. The wife had taken to accompanying a brood of ducklings, which Luke had hatched in the incubator before we left, on outings around the farm. They were kept with the chickens in a little sectioned-off space with a tub for paddling, and we had left instructions to keep them there. Perhaps the wife felt this wasn't particularly exciting for them, so she started walking them daily, acting as their nanny as the ducks explored further afield. On this particular afternoon, she had popped back to the house to grab a book/go to the loo/ have a glass of water. When she returned, she found half of her brood slain. Whether it was a fox or an eagle, the assassin was unknown. The wife was beside herself, and despite our assurances that these things happened, she couldn't bear to stay there any longer. With my sister's pre-wedding dinner taking place within hours, we begged them to hold on. Fortunately, the husband managed to persuade his wife to see it through, and they did. But we made a note that for any future interviews with house sitters, we needed to confirm their tolerance of animal death.

Chapter 18

Rameses

Back home it wasn't just ducks we were down. The beehives, having survived the storm, had sadly succumbed to another. An invasive species with an insatiable appetite for the honeybee, the Asian Hornet was believed to have arrived in a shipment of pottery from Southeast Asia in 2010.

Jack was also battling the Asian Hornet and had taken to sitting by his hives with an electric fly swat (the type that looks like a tennis racket) and killing them as they approached. But with a new baby and an old farm, we just didn't have the time for this method. We tried the traps, but they were indiscriminate with what they trapped, and so we'd quickly ruled them out. The only thing that deterred them for a little while was the anti-Asian Hornet boxes that attached to the entrance of the hives. The Asian Hornet used two methods for catching the honeybee. If the hive was weak, or if the Hornet was feeling bold, then they would infiltrate the hive and gorge on the larvae. The anti-Asian Hornet boxes were designed so that the honeybees could still pass through the slats, but the Asian Hornet could not, thus stopping them from this first method of attack. However, the Asian Hornets just adapted their hunting technique, instead hovering in front of the hives and picking off the honeybees individually. A single hornet had been shown to kill as many as forty bees per minute. A group of thirty hornets would wipe out an entire hive (of approximately 30,000) bees in less than four hours.

In 2012, honeybee losses reached 30% in the Basque area of Pasaia Donibane, and closer to home, El Mexicano's son had lost thirty of his ninety hives over the summer. It was predicted that the Asian Hornet would have taken over the rest of the country by the end of the decade.

The local ayuntamiento (town hall) would come out and destroy Asian Hornet nests if called, but we never found a nest. And so, whilst losing the bees was upsetting, with no clear idea of how to combat the Asian Hornets, we decided not to replace them. And a few days after they'd been cleared away, Olaya told us over coffee that she was very pleased they were gone. Having them so close to her land made her feel uncomfortable. And, whilst she was on the subject, where we'd put them was illegal. Beehives should not be within two hundred metres of private land and/or footpaths, and we'd broken both those laws with our hive placement. We asked that in future she told us immediately if we did anything that made her unhappy. Neighbourly feuds were rife in the village, we'd been warned of many, he said she said sort of stuff, of which Olaya was the source of her fair share, and we were keen not to enter into any ourselves.

We may have been down on bees, but we were up on sheep, for we'd been gifted a ram. We'd made the decision to grow our flock, from the four we currently had, three ewes and one little castrated male, and we'd decided to keep with the same breed. They were an ancient Asturian race of mountain sheep, called Xalda. The history of the Xalda sheep dates back to 27 BC when Estrabon, the Greek geographer and historian, wrote of black tunics made by members of the Asturi tribe from the wool of the Xalda. The Asturian's were fiercely proud of them and keeping them felt like a good way to ingratiate us with the locals. On top of that they were hardy, and their ability to feed on almost anything was impressive. They'd nibble on nettles, chew bramble tips and browse the gorse. We'd put the word out for a ram and a neighbour got in touch and offered for us to go and choose one of last year's boys from his flock, before he sent them off for slaughter. The chosen one was named Rameses, and we calculated that if he ruffled a few fleeces promptly we could expect some lambs by the spring.

But first Rameses decided to escape the top field he'd been released into with his new flock and lead them on a wild goose chase into the monte above Wild Finca. Luke had gone to retrieve them and found that sadly one of the old ewes gifted by Angel was caught in between two rocks, her leg broken. He carried her down, we called El Mexicano's son for help and he came around to teach us how to despatch the ewe. The Asturian way turned out to be a rock to the head, not the swiftest of endings, and then EL Mexicano's son helped us to butcher her.

I should probably jump back just a little bit here and acknowledge the fact that when Luke and I first arrived in Asturias we'd both been vegetarian. Triggered during our time travelling, when we'd covered stories where prime wildlife habitat was being cleared for grazing animals, and too many animals were being kept and killed in inhumane conditions, we'd come to the decision that we were no longer comfortable eating meat that we couldn't source. However, we were starting to see that perhaps there was a way for meat to be produced ethically and in a manner that benefited the environment, and so more recently we'd begun eating meat again. Not regularly, and always sourced from local farmers and butchers that came recommended. We'd also started eating our own chickens, so with a perfectly healthy ewe struck down due to injury we were not going to let good mutton go to waste. And thank goodness we didn't, the meat had been a game changer for us. The moment we served our first Wild Finca sheep with a vegetable medley from the garden, well food had never tasted better. Being able to produce our own meat, knowing exactly its journey from field to fork, was what it was all about. And that they could help benefit the wildlife at Wild Finca, it felt like they had been perfectly designed for the Wild Finca vision. We knew that we would be producing our own from herein out, we just needed to come up with a smoother process than the rock method.

We did try to keep up with our filming of the wolf. By we, I mean Luke. We agreed that a few days away for Luke filming, every now and then, wouldn't hurt work at Wild Finca. And just when I started to feel confident alone with Roan, Luke arranged to meet Pablo who had a late wolf den with cubs. They'd met at silly o'clock in the morning, Luke leaving the Skidonk in the local town where Pablo lived, and Pablo driving them both up to where the hike to the den began. Pablo told Luke about a picturesque spot where the wolves were passing through daily, to and from the den, and he'd set off with directions with the plan for Pablo to head to a spot on the opposite mountainside from where he could see the den. Luke was perhaps ten minutes into his walk when out of the gloom two very aggressive mastíns bounded toward him. He ran and jumped a fence, ripping his trousers on the barbed wire as he went. Perhaps a better result than what would've happened had the mastíns reached him.

Luke had called Pablo who'd directed him away down another track, destined for a mammal crossing point at a river, with the advice to always carry a rock in case of further encounters with angry dogs. After countless run-ins with mastíns over his years wolf-watching, Pablo had found that the threat of a rock being thrown always proved enough to dissuade a full-blown attack. The problem now was that Luke needed to get to the new spot without disturbing any potential wolves, and he didn't have long before sunrise. It was misty and damp, and straight away Luke saw fresh wolf tracks. Then, ahead of him, a figure emerged, perhaps a rock, but as he raised his binoculars the rock began to move away from him. He was walking in the literal footsteps of a wolf. In the mist it was hard to get a clear view, and the wolf dropped off the track before disappearing into the scrub below. Luke followed quietly behind and below the scrub where the wolf had disappeared, Luke found the river, and a natural weir, just as Pablo had described. The wolf must have crossed for there was now no sign of it. There Luke set up camp and hoped it or others might return soon.

An hour later I called. I am told I was incoherent. But finally, Luke made some sense of my words. Roan had rolled off the bed, landed on his head and wouldn't stop screaming. I was on my way to the hospital, and I needed Luke. Now.

Of course, Roan was fine, and, of course, an hour after Luke got to us Pablo had messaged to say that from the valley opposite he'd watched through his scope as four wolves passed over the very crossing point Luke had been stationed at. They would have walked right past Luke if he'd still been there.

Chapter 19

Surviving Winter

The first winter at Wild Finca was bitterly cold, mainly a result of some inexperienced decisions I'd made during my stint as project manager of the conversion. The first mistake, the purchase of a fire too small to heat the whole space. The second, to not stock up on wood for the winter with enough time for the wood to season, and so we'd bought green logs late, just as winter arrived, and they wouldn't burn hot. The third, and arguably the silliest, was to have allowed the builder to make the decision on whether or not to insulate the roof. The roof was made of asbestos, and, in all our defences, we were trying our best to do as little with it as possible. A new roof was inevitable, when we'd the money and the time. But who knew when that would be, and so the builder suggested a cork paint for the inside of the asbestos sheeting, which we'd gone for. However, once painted on it was barely a couple of centimetres coverage, so would surely offer little additional insulation. And so, before they began plaster boarding the stud walls, the builder had asked if we wanted more insulation. I asked the builder what he thought. 'Well, it's really warm in there when we are working,' he'd answered, 'so I would suggest you're okay without additional insulation.' If you think so, said I. Oh, boy, were we a clueless pair. On trying to work out why we were roasting all summer and had icicles forming on the windows in winter, (neither an ideal situation with a baby), I'd relayed the conversation to Luke, who'd slapped his hand against his forehead.

As well as the cold we faced back-to-back storms, which rattled our roof so severely I thought it would take off. I was so fearful that the giant pine, that overshadowed our bedroom, and the giant pear, that faced the spare room, would topple and come crashing through the roof, that on a couple of occasions, in the middle of the night, I'd moved everyone to the sitting room at the centre of the building. My theory was that if either tree was to fall, they wouldn't reach us there. When storm Amelie hit, (such a pretty name for something so terrifying), after a sleepless night, we emerged the next morning to find trees down across Wild Finca. And my previous theory had proved true; the giant pear was a few limbs lighter, those lost now laid precariously near to our house. There was also a large old walnut down across the green route, blocking the entire path. Luke spent the morning chopping it up and wheeling it back to store for next winter – at least we wouldn't be caught with unseasoned wood for the fire next year, a silver lining to the rest of the carnage. From then on, the morning after any storm, Luke took to putting the chainsaw in the back of the car, for he'd also been called upon to clear the road down to town from the village. A good excuse to get in the good books of our neighbours, and fill the wood store.

To counteract the winds, we began planting windbreaks to build up protection around Wild Finca. In areas of poor soil, we planted native saplings, and all along the fence line in the food forest we planted Common Hazel and Black Alder, not only to act as a windbreak but also that potentially they could be coppiced for firewood. And perhaps, best of all, in the hope that they would provide food for all manner of wildlife, especially for the Red Squirrels, who we knew lived locally and who Roan and I had seen for the very first time at the beginning of the month, during our local walk, which we called the Loop. To maybe one day in the future feeding the Cantabrian Brown Bear that was predicted to return. It was nice to think that work we were doing to protect ourselves also provided for wildlife.

Then Luke had gone away, and I'd been faced with two rather stressful encounters.

The first occurred whilst sat on the mound with Roan. I'd seen a man in high-vis with two dogs worrying the scrub at the heart of Wild Finca. I'd gone down to have a word, Roan hitched on my hip. I explained that this was private land and not for hunting. It had undoubtedly been poor Spanish, but it was a relatively simple sentence, and I was confident I had delivered my message understandably enough. He replied very clearly that if I had a problem with him being there, then I was going to have to call the police. The encounter left me feeling shaken. To know that a man with a gun could just turn up at my home and roam around it as he wished, made me feel incredibly uncomfortable. Clearly whoever we'd contacted via the number we'd been given had not passed on our message, and so the hunters kept coming.

The second incident began as we'd been sat in front of the lukewarm fire, the rain loud against the roof, a distinct damp patch appearing on the ceiling of our bedroom where an obvious leak had broken through, when our Workaway shouted from the kitchen sink, 'Katie, the ducks.' Just ignore her, I shouted, just shoo her away. One of the female Muscovy ducks had taken to flying up to our window to demand food. Who knew Muscovy ducks could fly!

'No, you should come, the ducks don't look very happy.' And she was correct, the ducks weren't very happy at all. They were dead and just as I had made it to the kitchen sink window, I saw a little brown tail disappear up the driveway.

I ran out into the torrential rain, following the direction the tail had vanished in, past fallen ducks, and up to the food forest where a dog was continuing its massacre of the ducks. Tail wagging it came to me as soon as I shouted, before cowering submissively at my feet. I grabbed it by the scruff, it was a small dog, long, brown and terrier like. I walked it back down past the route of its destruction and shut it in the hórreo. I then rang Luke. 'We have a problem; a dog has killed a load of our ducks.'

I sent him through a picture of the dog. He identified that it was someone's from the village, a man named Inacio, who regularly visited Olaya for whisky disguised as coffee. I knew him to wave at, a very cheery fellow, Inacio was one of the few that would always greet us when we passed. Luke messaged Olaya's grandson Mario (Olaya didn't have a mobile phone) to ask him if he could let Inacio know that we had his dog. In the meantime, I found two more duck bodies down by the chicken coop, the surviving ducks hiding with the chickens in their coop.

Inacio arrived a little while later, just as I'd finished collecting the still warm bodies of the seven ducks, and he began by getting his excuses in. The ducks were on the road, on the pathway, they were anywhere but on our land. My Spanish wasn't good enough to tell him that every one of the dead ducks I'd collected well within the boundaries of Wild Finca, and that I'd caught his dog red-pawed with its last victim in the food forest. He finally admitted that his dog had never seen ducks before, so that must be why it had gone on its killing spree. Chickens she was fine with, but ducks not so much. He asked me if I was going to eat the ducks. I said (with a lot of gesturing to help explain my muddled Spanish) that I would try, but with just me and the baby, and a vegetarian Workaway, seven ducks were quite a big meal. As Inacio left he muttered something about compensation, and rabbits, but we were not going to chase it, whatever he'd meant, for risk of misunderstanding the offer and starting a rift with a neighbour. There was a lot of fault lines through the village, and we were conscious not to create any ourselves. I was sad about the loss, but I was more annoyed that so many had been taken by someone's pet. Wild animals predating our animals, that I could understand, but someone's pet killing for fun was something I couldn't accept.

However, I wasn't going to waste their lives, and once Inacio was gone I hung the ducks in the old farmhouse fridge and called Ali, who came over the next day to help me butcher them. I knew how to dress a pheasant, my grandad would always bring home a brace after a day with his local shoot, and he had taught me how to prepare them, but it'd been a while, and my recently ended stretch as a vegetarian had made me a little rusty, so I was thankful for Ali's guidance.

Meanwhile, from Ireland, where Luke was filming, he'd messaged Mario to ask what the protocol was for an incident like this. Mario had replied that 'of course this sort of thing will happen, you will just have to be careful'. Which was rather confusing as although the ducks were free-range, they did stay within our land boundaries. Fencing had taken a bit of a backseat, for as well as the cost, we wanted wildlife to be able to come and go freely, and so we were still figuring out what to do about that. When Luke returned home, we decided it was time to get a dog.

It didn't take long for a puppy to be found. The mother was an abandoned hunting dog, a beautiful wire-haired Griffon Bleu, found wandering collarless at the end of the hunting season, just one of an epidemic of discarded hunting dogs. She'd been taken in just in time for her puppies to be born. Three remained by the time we visited, two boys and a girl, and it was the girl that instantly bonded with our little family. The owner had named her Indie, as she was very independent in comparison to her brothers, and we decided to keep it. Indie came home with us that same day.

Chapter 20

Goat Rage

When the rain stopped the work began, and no one was safe to visit without being put to work. My dad spent one trip cementing the bottom of the hórreo, with the vision of it becoming a cold storeroom. After the next big rains it had flooded, proving perhaps why it hadn't been cemented in the first place. To rule out a leak from the garage, that attached to the hórreo, Luke took advantage of a longer stretch of dry to retile the garage roof. Full of rotten planks, it was rather amazing it hadn't collapsed under the deluge. But given how when the rains came, they really came, had Luke not fixed the roof it would have surely only been a matter of time before it fell.

Indie settled in quickly, she was a sweet, loving little dog. All the local hunters had a particularly soft spot for her, and we had many tell us what a fine dog she was. One even stopping us on a walk of the Loop to offer to buy her from us. Unfortunately, she turned out not to be a very good guard dog. Her instinct to kill was too strong, and she saw her wards more as quarry. After her first kill we kept her close to hand, scolding her if she ever chased any of the chickens or ducks. But the most damage was done at the beginning of December, during our visit to the UK. Wild Finca had been left in the hands of a 'professional housesitter', named Phoebe. Phoebe assured us that if in the unfortunate event there was a casualty, she wouldn't abandon us. However, that was because Phoebe wasn't very present, and so she was completely oblivious to the fact that there had been any casualties at all.

Phoebe worked remotely at night and then when she'd finished her work, sometime in the early hours of the morning, she would kick Indie out before going to bed herself. Indie was then left to her own devices for the best part of the day, and we returned to half the number of chickens than we'd left. Meanwhile Phoebe had no idea of the losses, and clearly hadn't left the house much, bar walking the path down to the chickens to put them in at night and let them out the next morning, for most of the chicken's bodies remained a stone's throw from the front step and said pathway. As for the house, Phoebe wasn't comfortable making the fire, and the week we were away it'd rained pretty much non-stop (which does explain her not leaving the house much, to be fair). I'm sure there would have been issues regardless of whether or not the pitiful fire had been going during our absence, but without the fire, and the fact Phoebe had kept all of the curtains closed, the mould that covered all four walls in our bedroom was thick by the time we got home. The smell of it hit us the moment we'd stepped in. We moved into the spare room, where Phoebe had slept, which was slightly better for having been lived in. And Luke went out and bought a new fire. It took two weeks to make the bedroom liveable again, but we continued to find patches of mould all over the house for months afterwards. The roof became a priority after that and went to the top of the to-do list for when the weather was good enough.

Taking on a project like Wild Finca came with a never-ending to-do list, and a job that joined the roof at the top of the to-do list was to sort the electricity. Clearly our energy needs far exceeded that of the BFG's, and as the winter had ramped up, so we began to experience more and more outages. We'd applied to increase our supply, but as we were coming to learn, nothing happens quickly here, and so we saw in the New Year by fire and candlelight.

In the anticipation of increased wattage, we'd ordered a drier. We were using washable nappies with Roan, certainly the new fire had made the system quicker, for the nappies that I had hanging above it dried quicker, but overall, I was struggling to keep on top of laundry having to dry everything inside by the fire. There was a small building attached below where we lived, where we already had the washing machine, but which needed new doors. A carpenter came to measure up the job and declared he had just the thing in his workshop in Ponga, and so we headed over one afternoon to look. Ponga is a beautiful natural park just under an hour's drive from us. More than a third of it is made up of mature forests of European Beech, English Oak, Silver Birch, European Ash and Black Alder. The carpenter specialised in restoring hórreos and was particularly passionate about bringing new life to old wood. He lived, we felt, in very appropriate surroundings.

The drive up was delayed thanks to the usual Asturian roadblock, cattle traffic. But a little late still means on time in Spain, and as we were on time we still had to wait the mandatory twenty minutes for the carpenter to turn up. No matter, the views from his workshop were spectacular, and when he arrived the heavy old chestnut doors he had in mind were perfect. We bought them, he agreed to deliver and fit them the following week, and we also left with a few offcuts of wood that had knots perfectly placed to make bird boxes.

Alongside Wild Finca work we were also taking some time to explore what sort of living we could make on the ground. And so, on the night of the Wolf Moon (the full moon at the end of January, named such for it is believed wolves were more likely to be heard howling at this time), we headed up to the Picos. Pablo had told us wolves were being seen and heard by the Lagos de Covadonga and so we'd gone to listen for howling. Luke was also starting to get enquiries about leading nature tours in the area, and we felt this experience could be a unique one to offer. It was bitterly cold, but we wrapped up in snow suits and went armed with soup, cake and hot tea. The night was clear, the full moon bright, and we found a spot to settle ourselves down to wait. Suddenly Luke began howling, like Pablo had done that first time, and equally as wolf-like (clearly, he'd been practising). And after a beat, a howling erupted amongst us. Not a wolf, but poor Roan who'd been given such a fright he'd burst into inconsolable sobbing. He was so distraught we ended up having to call it a night. Between the crying baby and the icy weather, it was unlikely we were going to get wolves that evening. But the experience itself had been magical, definitely one to develop further.

And then, on 31 January, a day we never thought would come, did. After three previous dates came and went, the dreaded Brexit day finally came, and with it the end of the UK's membership of the European Union. We'd invited Spanish friends over for the evening to toast a sad farewell. A short-sighted move, in our opinion, but fortunately Luke and I had our residency sorted, and Roan had been born in Spain, so he was okay... 'were we sure about that?' Our friends asked. 'Pretty sure...' we'd replied. But it sowed a seed of doubt, and sure enough when we checked up on it, we learnt that we should have applied for Roan's residency when he'd been born. Without the paperwork, he was essentially an illegal immigrant. We contacted a solicitor immediately who said they would start the process but with the new situation it could take up to six months, and there was a chance he could still be rejected.

On top of the bureaucracy, we now faced, Roan was diagnosed with a suspected heart murmur, and they'd referred him to the hospital in the city. Fortunately, the referral was much quicker than the residency application and he was seen to and given the all clear within the month. To celebrate we'd stopped by the local dog shelter and left with a friend for Indie, and hopefully a better guard dog for all our animals, a mastín cross mongrel pup who we called Otis.

To take our mind off the bureaucracy we now faced, we focussed on Wild Finca, drawing on our successes and failures of our first year so far, and seeing how we could learn from them as we moved forward. Sadly, our biggest failure proved to be the goats. We had been giving them free rein around the farm again after the roof tiles, that hung precariously between the rafters above 'the goat palace', had started to come down by the dozen during the storms. In true Pan and Coco style they'd taken advantage of their free rein, knocking twenty brand-new tiles off the only just re-fitted hórreo roof. But breaking point came the day after.

Our young food forest may have survived the rain and the valley's bracing winds, and with the geese and ducks now keeping the grass down it was even starting to flourish. That was until Pan and Coco got in. They had done so before, but this time we didn't realise before it was too late. Now Luke's quite a relaxed chap, it's a comment often made about his disposition, but on seeing the snapped saplings that littered the food forest, I am not sure I have ever seen him that angry before or since. Our friends, who also kept goats, called it 'goat rage' and Luke's 'goat rage' got the better of him. A new home needed to be found for the pair, and it didn't take much persuading for me to agree. Pan had recently head butted a friend's three-year-old daughter. Luckily, he hadn't done any serious damage, beyond shock, but he could have. And after that I'd noticed he did have a particular aversion to small humans, which made me concerned for our own small human. Fortunately, El Mexicano's son was looking for some bramble mowers, and our two goats fitted the role perfectly.

Meanwhile our biggest success was proving to be the sheep, particularly their resilience through the winter. Growing up, my grandparents had kept a small flock of hobby sheep, Southdowns if I recall correctly, and I'd become used to watching them in their putting-green-like fields; short, cropped grass with little to no diversity. So, to now keep sheep who thrived in a varied habitat of grasses and shrubs was a whole new learning experience. There were many differences between those sheep of my grandparents and our Xaldas that went beyond their grazing habits. My grandad used to joke that sheep were born wanting to die; they would do everything in their power to kill themselves. Stuck on their back? May as well die. Fell in a ditch? Better to just die. Something scary? I'm going to drop dead. But this behaviour, well documented amongst people who keep sheep, is actually down to breeding. In stark contrast our native little sheep were robust, and it took a lot to kill them. At the end of February Rameses proved his virility by siring twin lambs. Hopefully our second ewe would also have a lamb by Rameses this season, but even after that we planned to expand the flock once we were back from our holiday.

Chapter 21

Covid-19

For us, it began the first weekend of March 2020. We'd picked up our house sitter, Elias, and were showing him the ropes. We'd been relieved to see that he appeared completely capable of managing our menagerie. His day was normal (as in he was up and about during daylight hours) and he didn't seem concerned by the idea that a death might occur (ideally not, of course) but that if it were to, we felt confident he wouldn't disappear. Then at 5 a.m. the following morning, with minor apprehension from what the news was saying, we got in the car and headed to the French Alps.

The plan was to slowly make our way there, where we would meet my parents, before heading back to the UK for my cousin's wedding, and then return two days later with my brother, sister and her husband for a weeklong family holiday.

The drive took three days and en route we'd stopped at friends of ours in the South of France, who'd just taken on a similar property to Wild Finca. Their philosophy was that all work needed to be respectful to nature, inclusive and fun. Roan sat on his first pony there, a little black Shetland called Prince, who'd calmly walked around the paddock, to the delight of Roan, his chubby cheeks jiggling with joy.

It was a wonderful stop off, but there was an undertone of nervousness throughout the visit. The reports of the Covid-19 virus that'd been wreaking havoc on the other side of the world was now starting to tear through Europe. The doubts as to whether we should be cancelling our trip and turning around at that point began to creep in. But while some of the reports looked ominous for what was to come, others dismissed it all as hysteria. Certainly, what we were reading in the UK underplayed the whole situation, whilst it was the news from Europe we should have heeded. But I was desperate to make it to my dearest cousin's wedding, which was being held at my grandparents' house, the ceremony set to take place in the same local church where my parents had married. I was excited to see extended family and introduce them to Roan. Despite living abroad and travelling a lot I am close to my family, and the thought of us all being together for the first time in a long time filled me with joy.

By the time we arrived in the Alps, the headlines were still a melee and the doubts about our decision to continue got stronger. We spent the evening with my parents, all still pretending we would be getting on our flight the next day to the UK, but when I woke the next morning Luke was already up and he finally put his foot down. 'We aren't going to the wedding,' he said, 'and tomorrow, we need to go home.'

It was of course the only decision there was. Covid figures were ramping up by the hour, and threats of border closures were being made. On top of that Luke, was sniffling. He'd returned only the week before from a UK-wide tour working for Sony, where he'd shaken a lot of people's hands in the process. It was a horrible phone call to make to my cousin the morning before her wedding, but she was also high risk and completely understood our reasons.

After saying goodbye to my parents, who'd pressed on, we walked in the forest, we watched a movie in the snug, we even went for a drink in one of the local bars. And then suddenly, things started moving very quickly, and decisions that affected us were being made with lightning speed. France was closing all non-essential establishments the very next day. Followed by Spain declaring a nationwide lockdown to also begin the following day.

On the morning of Sunday the fifteenth, we began the thirteen-hour journey across France towards home. We could not do it in one hit with Roan, and so we stayed with our same friends halfway. Luke and I were both apprehensive as we crossed the border the following day, fearing we'd be stopped and questioned as to why we were on the road. A new rule that only one person per car was allowed had also been introduced, but fortunately we didn't have any trouble. A few road signs flashed up along our route with reminders that we were in a state of emergency and that travel was prohibited unless justified. Other than that, the roads were dead, and there was no police presence to be seen.

Elias made the decision to hang tight with us at the farm. He moved into the hórreo, which fortunately had been somewhat upgraded since the BFG moved out. The roof repaired and insulated, the old sacks stuffed into the holes in the wall removed and replaced with glass. The old smoke room knocked through so that it was now one room inside with a sofa bed. Cosy but still very basic, and as we'd agreed to keep our distance for the week, just in case we'd caught it on our journey, it meant Elias had to cook on a BBQ outside. By this point Luke was beginning to deteriorate, and his brother-in-law, who he'd stayed with during his Sony tour, had just tested positive. I was beginning to get so panicky about Roan and Luke getting it. Going on what the news reports were telling us, Ro was the least likely to get it, but with Luke's asthma, he was in the high-risk category. Luke certainly came down with something, but exactly what we never knew for sure. We were fortunate that whatever it was it was mild, and Ro and I didn't get it.

The lockdown was supposed to last two weeks, but as the date for its end drew closer it became clearer that this was going to last a lot longer. Friends and family asked us how we were coping under the Spanish lockdown rules, and the truth was we were doing just fine.

Chapter 22

The Birth of the Vegetable Patch

Word of food shortages was rife and so we'd started rationing the chicken grain, which they were very unimpressed with and started joining the female Muscovy on the kitchen windowsill to demonstrate their indignation. They were free range so didn't really have an excuse for their protests. It wasn't just animal food shortages that were being warned of, but for us too. To date we had made tentative starts on a vegetable patch, but lockdown gave us the time to really commit to it.

When we first moved to Wild Finca, whilst still deciding where to put our veggie garden, we'd bought a large plastic greenhouse which we'd erected down in the chicken area. We planted some tomatoes and aubergines in it, but Luke had been away filming, I was heavily pregnant with Roan, and they'd been forgotten about. When I finally went to check them, they were gone, the slugs had barely left a leaf. Before we'd a chance to re-plant it Storm Amelie had ripped the greenhouse from its roots and the next morning, we'd found it the other side of Wild Finca. It was packed away and only more recently been resurrected on the prow just above the garage, at the edge of what was being transformed into the vegetable garden.

The whole plot for the vegetable garden was around 140m², situated on the raised land opposite the old farmhouse. It was close to our barn, got sun all day long, and all year round. The only drawback was that it was a little exposed; with the views down both valleys that intersect at Wild Finca, come some ferocious winds. Luke aimed to counter this with raised beds and, with the help of some Workaways, he'd begun building some out of old pallets salvaged from the builders' merchants. However, the beds had remained empty since creation, for although Olaya's tenant farmer had said we could have the manure from Olaya's barn (where he kept some of his cows during the winter months), we just hadn't had the time to take him up on his offer. Now with the pandemic, we had all the time. And so, while Luke set to work redesigning the landscape with more raised beds, thanks to Elias, our house-sitter turned Workaway (due to our new living situation), the raised beds were slowly being filled with aged manure collected from Olaya's barn.

You are probably thinking 'poor Elias', but luckily for us Elias was a fit chap who was missing the gym-life. Plus, after a neighbour visiting their land mentioned that our 'guest' (already a frowned upon concept given the circumstances) running the Loop could not be considered within the current restrictions (Spain's lockdown was declared the strictest imposed of any country and people weren't even allowed out to exercise), our imaginative cardio suggestion was surprisingly well received.

One day, Elias was returning from Olaya's barn, his barrow full of poo, when he told us that he'd just met Olaya's son. That Olaya even had a son was news to us. We knew she had a daughter who lived with Olaya's sister in the top village. Word on the village grapevine was that she didn't talk to her daughter, but she did have a relationship with her sister, and she would often drive up to visit. Finding Olaya behind the wheel of a car was a terrifying experience, that often ended up with her having to reverse, having been so far over the wrong side of the road that there was no way she could have rectified her current course. One time she came so close to reversing off the side of the road and down a gulley, that from her angle, a back wheel must have surely been hanging in thin air. Luke had told me to go and offer to help. I did no such a thing, had I done that I imagine I would have been killed. Somehow her car had stayed on the road, we had passed, and she had miraculously got her car back on the road and continued up the hill.

Olaya also had two grandsons (or nephews) who she often talked of, but as she had never mentioned their parents, and knowing her daughter didn't have children, I had convinced myself that they must be her nephews (even though she had used the Spanish word for grandson 'nieto' – although you can see my confusion). Ultimately, no son had ever been mentioned by Olaya or the village grapevine.

Apparently, the son had seemed bemused by the tall, dark, shirtless man seemingly stealing cow shit from beneath his mother's house. So, Luke did the next run to explain what was going on, and check Olaya was okay and hadn't been infiltrated by a squatter.

He came back and confirmed that Alberto, Olaya's son, the father of her two grandchildren was indeed home. From where, we had no idea, by the time Luke visited there was a little pile of beer cans and so he'd kept the conversation short and sweet. But he'd spied Olaya busy in her kitchen through the open window, clearly not being held under duress.

With the beds filling nicely, soon we were planting out soft fruits we'd brought back from our friends in France; raspberry, loganberries, red and blackcurrants, and transferring some of our seedlings of kale, spinach, leeks, beetroots and carrots, into our new vegetable patch. At the end of March, we spent Luke's mum's birthday sowing more seeds. Luke's mum passed in 2016 and had been looking for a way to commemorate her. Luke told me a story about how his mum used to have an old ice cream tub filled with seeds, which she kept under the stairs, and on weekends he and his sisters would go through it choosing what they were going to plant next. Since arriving in Asturias, I'd been in awe of Luke's gardening knowledge, and despite the sheep's break-ins we'd enjoyed endless punnets of raspberries, rainbow chard and spinach galore. We managed a fair few aubergines in a little plastic greenhouse we invested in, (but that did not survive the winter winds, and we should have learnt our lesson at that point not to purchase a plastic greenhouse again). And then, last November at the rental, on returning from our long travel stint, we had come home to enough butternut squashes to feed an army. They had lasted us the winter and beyond. Luke had a way of making this growing business look easy.

For Luke, being outside, either in nature or working in the garden was his comfort through the grief of losing his mum, and although celebrating someone's life doesn't need to be allocated to just one day, for us it was a nice way to remember Tracey and introduce her to Roan. It was also incredibly important to us that Roan learnt these skills, which we felt were only becoming more important.

And so, on our first 'Nana Tracey Seed Planting Day', we sowed basil, parsley, cucamelons (a miniature cucumber crossed with a watermelon), pickling cucumbers, kalettes, tomatoes, melons, butternut squash, gem squashes and courgettes. We didn't do a great job of labelling them so when they came up, it was a guessing game as to what each one was. We also planted wildflower strips around the edge of the garden, a mixture of those that'd been gifts from Tracey's funeral, and favours from my sister's wedding the previous summer.

All the while Roan loved being in the garden, searching for worms, hands deep in the soil, throwing odd fistfuls of the stuff in the air. Tired from such activities, he would then lie with the dogs on the picnic table as Luke and I planted out seedlings.

Chapter 23

Our First Spring at Wild Finca

A cold snap hit at the end of March, and a hailstorm knocked the giant pear tree for six. Blossom fell like snow on the chicken area and covered the pond. We put our two beehives out in the hope of catching a passing swarm. We set up one of the beehives on the stretch of land we'd named the Snake Pit (due to the success our reptile mats had there for attracting Seoanei's Viper, Smooth Snake and Grass Snake). The second beehive we set up on a spot we had called Los Pinos, a scrubby strip in the centre of Wild Finca we'd named such for the two large pines which had been planted by the BFG's family sixty years ago. Both were as far as possible from Olaya, and where the beehives had previously been located Luke was now building a compost bin. We checked the hives regularly on our walks of the finca, the two at the Snake Pit were easy to access but the third we would check with our binoculars, for access was tricky through the growing tangle of brambles that surrounded Los Pinos. Disappointingly they'd all remained empty.

The Short-toed Eagles arrived and could be seen hovering over the fields in search of snakes. A pair of Egyptian Vultures came next and, to our delight, would fly by each afternoon. But the migrants that gave us perhaps the most joy were the Red-backed Shrike pair that arrived, stayed and nested. We'd seen them around, but to have a nesting pair on our farm was overwhelmingly exciting. Known for skewering their prey on thorny vegetation, or even barbed wire fences, their Latin name Lanius translates as butcher, and in some areas, they are known as 'butcher birds'. They're such a charismatic little bird, whose range is sadly declining across Europe. This is mainly due to habitat changes and intensification of agriculture, as the shrub they so favour for their nesting continues to be ripped out.

The second of the remaining ewes had a lamb. Five Griffon Vultures watched over, waiting for their moment to clear the placenta, the clean-up crew on duty. We'd named the ewe Old Mamma, due to the fact that her passport stated she was sixteen! Although more likely Old Mamma had just inherited another sheep's passport, which was a usual way of shortcutting paperwork and keeping a sheep here and there for your own use. The latter explanation was more likely given how easily she birthed and how sturdy her little male lamb was.

Throughout the day, Old Mamma kept her young lamb hidden away in Los Pinos and she'd only bring him out when we fed them in the afternoons. The feeding was done not out of necessity, for there was more than enough grazing, but to get the sheep bucket trained. For whilst they did not escape, they also wouldn't follow which was making moving them quite tricky and, at times, Luke had resorted to carrying them one by one to where he wanted them to go. Not the most efficient method, and if we wanted to increase the flock size this certainly wouldn't have worked long term.

The eggs we'd collected from our friends in France, and popped under two broody chickens, all hatched, and along with a surprise nest we ended up with around thirty chicks. Cuckoo flowers began to appear across the fields, a little early for they are supposed to arrive with the Cuckoo, but he was surely still in the Congo. We snacked on the yellow coconut flavoured flowers of the gorse bushes. We learnt that the abundance of mole hills across our land was in fact a good sign, for moles are natural aerators of soil. Their underground tunnels loosen soil and form channels for air and water to move freely through the soil, which helps plants to growth.

The nettle beds, which we'd been getting stick from the locals about for they insisted we needed to herbicide them, erupted in writhing masses of Peacock Butterfly larvae. Spiky little black caterpillars, covered in silver dots, munched their way through the patches. Nettles support more than forty species of insect, which in turn attract insect-eating birds and mammals. So, despite them not being as pretty as wildflowers, they more than have their worth.

We also began clearing one of the many rubbish dumps we'd found during our wanders of the land. One hidden amongst a hedge that lined the path to the meadows below, and a second beneath the large ash tree, were the first we attacked after they were uncovered by wildlife. Taking wheelbarrows of rubbish (old cider bottles, an old television with a smashed screen, endless plastic and empty packets of rat poison and vials of medicine for cattle) and replacing it with wood piles for insects and lizards. But after a while we realised it was a never-ending battle that we were losing, as new sites regularly became uncovered by storms and animals. Most of the rubbish sites were charred from when the piles got too big and would then be burnt. A practice Olaya and Alberto were still partaking in, the stench of acrid plastic becoming a regular monthly occurrence. Yet oddly enough these rather disgusting spots did still offer a home to a lot of invertebrates and reptiles. Glow Worms and Slow Worms could both be found in abundance amongst the debris.

Meanwhile, our routine trips to the nearest rubbish bins in the village became an excuse to catch up on what our neighbours were up to. And it offered an opportunity to deliver eggs to one neighbour we'd set up a barter arrangement with, who in exchange would leave either a bottle of wine or a fresh loaf of bread in a bag on their gate.

For the rest of the time, we got to know our land. Wild Finca sits along one side of a valley, and at the bottom of our boundary we join a beautiful old forest, some of the last remaining in our line of sight. Sadly, eucalyptus plantations make up many of the forested slopes that surround us, but that strip of old forest is vibrant in life, and our early camera traps on our border with it recorded Wild Boar, Roe Deer, European Badger, Red Fox, Pine Marten and even a Genet. During the day we would wander amongst the moss-covered beech, oak and chestnuts. Wood Sorrel and Horsetails grew in abundance, and we snacked on the bounty of Primroses. We were delighted to find Wood Anemones springing up like a galaxy of stars across the forest floor. They are a true sign of an ancient woodland and spread slowly (six feet in a hundred years), relying on the growth of their root structure rather than the spread of their seed. And down by the stream at the bottom of the woods we found a glut of Wild Garlic, which we turned into pesto, and cheese and wild garlic scones.

It was also during this time that the Self-Isolating Bird Club was set up, an online daily show documenting the wonders of wildlife as a tonic to the lockdowns. Luke sent in a short film of our dawn chorus, and it was so well received he became a regular contributor, sharing the magic of Wild Finca.

By late spring the veg patch was providing broccoli, chard, spinach and courgettes, all regulars on the menu. The only time anyone left the farm was for shopping essentials and, after Luke had recovered from his bout of whatever it was he'd caught in the UK, it tended to be him who did the shopping. On entering any shops we were made to disinfect our whole body, and everyone was made to wear face masks and gloves. It was on the way home from one of these shops that Luke had been stopped at a roadblock by the retired head of Police (brought out of retirement to help support the Covid measures). When he saw Luke's address on his identity card, the man smiled and he introduced himself as Jesús, owner of a little cabana just above us, and our second nearest neighbour. Jesús insisted Luke pop over for a sidra when restrictions allowed, and then Luke was waved on his way.

The only time anyone came to the farm was to visit land or move animals. At the centre of Wild Finca there was a hectare of land owned by an elderly chap named Ramiro. Ramiro lived in the main local town, but he also had a house in the village, as well as quite a bit of land scattered about. This particular plot he would graze on rotation with his two nephews; so, at any given time it was likely to have on it either sheep belonging to Ramiro, cows belonging to the one nephew, or horses belonging to the other nephew. To access the land, they could legally pass down through our front drive and past our farmhouse. When they had animals on the land they'd pass through daily. It could have been inconvenient, but the men were polite to us and kept us updated on the local goings on. The day the UK went into lockdown the owner came by to check on his nephew's pregnant horse that was due any day. We too had been keeping an eye on the horse, letting them know the status every time we walked the land.

In the end there was no need for us checking in for Ramiro and both nephews would be by numerous times a day, the activity giving them all an excuse to get out, and an opportunity to share a bit of local news. That day Ramiro was lamenting the lack of tobacco in town, apparently a victim of the disrupted supply chains. He'd passed on the news that a lady from Collia, the neighbouring village that could be reached via the footpath that crossed our land, had died from Covid. Her husband was in a critical state in hospital, and her daughter was ill too. They'd all caught the virus from the daughter, who'd brought it from Madrid. There'd been a huge influx of city folk escaping to their country holiday homes to sit out the lockdown, and local people were getting fearful that if it did all kick off in our local community, our rural hospitals wouldn't be able to cope.

Chapter 24

A Shift in Perspective

In the early days I would follow the news hourly, but I soon found it too difficult and after a while, I stopped. Yet, with the world essentially closed, there were good news stories to come from it all. With air travel grounded and people working from home, carbon emissions were down. And I saw tweets from Venice that their waterways had become so clear in the absence of boat traffic that you could see the fish in the canals, swans had returned and even dolphins had been spotted. Pablo messaged us stories he was hearing from the shepherds out tending to their flocks in the mountains; that sightings of bears and wolves were more frequent. With the reduced human presence, they were becoming bolder, exploring more in daylight, new behaviour, Pablo reported.

Then there was the flip side to these stories of nature bouncing back. From friends we'd worked with in Zambia they reported increased poaching due to the loss of tourism. Meanwhile in the Brazilian Pantanal fires were at an all-time high, as farmers cleared land for their cattle. With no income from tourism to protect the land, the wildlife was suffering. Without tourism, there was now no reason to look after land that had formerly been a tourist attraction.

Conversations of the gains and losses for nature, due to the Covid pandemic, were constant in our household. On the one hand we would find ourselves questioning our own carbon footprints, having spent the past five years telling global stories of wildlife. On the other hand, a lot of our work was promoting wildlife tourism, and with wildlife tourism came preservation and security of wildlife. We didn't have the answers, but we did know that the way we worked was going to have to adapt.

We took advantage of the time by getting to know our home more intimately, watching the Firecrests, Blue and Great Tits come and go from feeding in the giant pear tree, and back to their nest in the giant pine. Despite the threat I felt from both trees during a storm, they offered food and shelter to so many different species. It was such a pleasure hearing the first Grasshopper Warblers on our morning walks; shoo-ing the Swallows from our kitchen until the pair finally settled on making their nest under the hórreo; enjoying picnic dinners in the bottom field, watching the sea mist roll in, listening to the churr of Nightjars and watching them hawking over the opposite hillside, all the while discussing the future of Wild Finca, our working lives and if the two could ever become one and the same. Luke was still a hybrid wildlife photographer, cameraman and guide, still travelling a lot, but with one trip already cancelled for the summer who knew for how much longer there would be that sort of work. And irrelevant of Covid restrictions we'd been wanting to scale down the travel. Now with a young family we were having to do work trips alone, which wasn't as much fun. Meanwhile, I'd managed to pick up some freelance work as a marketing consultant, with a few writing projects on the side. Remote work, great as a parent and convenient too for the current climate. But could we ultimately marry our passion for protecting wildlife with our skillset, and our new home? Make Wild Finca our sole life's work, and make her pay for herself? This was our new goal, but we would only have managed this successfully if the monetary element was a by-product of a functioning ecological community. Never profit over biodiversity.

We were very aware that our local wildlife was as in need of protection as any of the wildlife we'd documented before. Our initial aim to do a story on the Iberian Wolf had already been undergoing a transformation since before Covid came along. We were being led away from investigative journalism as a way of trying to help the cause of the wolf and moving more towards nature tourism. Our motivation shifted from telling others the story (something we'd been doing for the past five years), to showing the locals the value of their iconic wildlife. Hoping to utilise Luke's nature guiding experience, but as proven by our encounter with the mayor of the local village of the denning wolves, current tourism models were not giving back and so if we were ever going to win people over to the wolf, we needed to find a way that it did.

Changing the perception of wildlife tourism was just one complex element that needed addressing. Another issue lay in the general attitude towards all wildlife. Whilst observing wildlife was our passion, it felt like a large portion of the local community's passion for wildlife extended only to killing it.

Since my run-in with the hunters, they had been a regular sight across the land; once a week, if we were lucky every other. The two main types of hunters that passed through Wild Finca were the boar hunters and the Woodcock hunters. The boar hunting was carried out in a way known as a driven hunt, where the men with guns set up in one location (up high and identifiable by their high-vis jackets) while large numbers of other men (I have only ever seen one woman on a hunt on our land) and packs of dogs move through the forest below, frightening the boar in the direction of the guns. Apparently, it is the oldest and most traditional form of hunting in Spain. I particularly enjoyed the direct Google translation of the official Asturias Hunting page of what a driven hunt, or 'batida', is, as the language seemed fitting for what we observed:

It is practised by gangs organised in two groups. One of them, that of the beaters or huntsmen, advances, harassing the pieces so that they leave their place of refuge or bed. The other, that of the hunters, is strategically located dominating the line of flight of the pieces to kill them.

The number of huntsmen and hunters depends on the characteristics of the hunting ground. In the Reserves, gangs of eight to twelve hunters are authorised, assisted by no more than six huntsmen who can be helped by a maximum of four dogs and must not carry any type of weapon. In the rest of the hunting grounds, gangs of eight to fifteen hunters are authorised, assisted by no more than ten huntsmen who can use a maximum of eight dogs.

On the whole, it describes what we experienced each hunt, although we regularly witnessed more dogs than was quoted. One claim I've heard from hunters is that they and their dogs are no different to a pack of wolves moving through the forest hunting. But the two are incomparable. Wolves are silent and focussed on their prey. Beaters and dogs are noisy and indiscriminate in what they disturb.

The second type of hunters were the woodcock hunters. More discreet at least, for they tended to go alone with their dogs. They'd use their dogs to search out the bird and put it up in the air for the hunter to shoot. But what made them potentially worse than the driven hunt was the chance of stumbling across them. For you rarely knew they were there until a shot had been fired. It made any walk in the woods during hunting season incomparably riskier.

And then, during the lockdown, hunters were declared 'essential workers', leaving them to go about their hunting business unquestioned. Meanwhile, the rest of us were given very little leeway for any sort of movement beyond our home confines.

Chapter 25

Freedom

Around Easter time Elias moved to Jack's Airbnb, which boasted a proper kitchen and being more remote than Wild Finca meant it was easier for Elias to get back to his running. On Easter Day a sack of rabbits arrived for us. They came as replacements for the duck massacre, and were delivered rather unceremoniously in a wriggling sack, dropped off by the nephew with the cows. Ramiro and Inacio were brothers-in-law, so they had the same nephews – we were quickly learning that everyone in the village was related in some shape or form. The nephew with cows was coming to check on his brother's horse which had given birth on the full moon, as predicted by all the men who had checked on it during that time. The two nephews' father (Inacio's half-brother, and Ramiro's half-brother in law), Raul, was perhaps the most outspoken on this full moon rule... and if I've lost you there on who's who, don't worry, I'm not entirely sure I've got their family tree in order yet myself.

Inside the bag were two black rabbits, a male and female. And so that afternoon's job quickly changed from whatever it had been to building a rabbit cage to accommodate them. An exercise that we proved unsuccessful at. The first enclosure we made for them, located within the chicken coop, they jumped out of. The second enclosure within a different section of the chicken coop, they dug themselves out of.

They were both lost in quick succession to the dogs, who would work themselves into a frenzy at the sight of them. We cooked the rabbits up (waste not, want not), and decided that rabbit was a brilliant source of protein, making a plan to collect some more after lockdown (the rabbits had come with an offer of more if wanted, for it was understood that two rabbits didn't quite equate to seven pedigree ducks).

As the temperatures rose the ponds took up a lot of Luke's attention, the lack of water becoming more noticeable, and nine months after it had been dug Luke lined the first pond, the one below the giant pear. Despite a wet winter the clay had not held the water, any rainwater initially caught had quickly drained, so both ponds were empty, bar a layer of sludge, and lining them became a necessity. It hadn't been a straightforward job. The first time Luke spent a day scraping it dry, with the intention of lining it the next morning, it proceeded to rain all night undoing all of Luke's hard work. Which meant he had to wait for more dry weather and go through the process of emptying it again. The chickens didn't mind, given all the goodies Luke uncovered for them.

With restrictions easing, we began to walk the Loop again. As described by its name, the Loop starts and ends at Wild Finca, but often, due to the gradients we tended to take the easier/less uphill route. Through the village, down the road at the back of the mountain to the neighbouring village, up the mountain path and back to Wild Finca via the green route. Along the way there are many fruit trees, and as they started to ripen, we'd go in search of fruit for a pie. Most times we'd return with barely enough to sustain us on the walk. The birds and mammals always got to the plums and cherries first, and Roan devoured the rest.

The green route runs alongside our top meadow which was now full of wildflowers, butterflies and bumblebees. Ticks too, the only downside to the long grass, and I kept forgetting to wear long trousers which meant returning covered in the little buggers. Food for someone I suppose.

Three months after it first began, the state of alarm ended on 21 June, and as soon as it did, we reached out to the neighbour from whom we got Rameses and asked to buy four more ewes.

Luke of course returned with five of last year's lambs. Four in the boot of the car and a fifth wedged in the footwell of the front passenger seat, (which had apparently been thrown in for free, due to it being a runt). But the fifth did not last long, for only a couple of days after they arrived, she had been killed.

It was after lunch, and we'd gone out to check on the animals. The first cause for concern was that there was no sign of the dogs. The second, that the gate that leads from the buildings through to the field the sheep were in had been forced open. We didn't have to go far into the field to find the dogs ripping chunks out of the little black and white ewe. At the sight of us the dogs ran, but it was too late, the sheep was in its death throes. We were horrified. We were completely responsible. We should have learnt from the rabbits. They were just puppies, following their instincts. They were at their very essence wolves; it was innate behaviour. But our lack of awareness, our lack of control, was the true culprit. We were losing more animals to domestic animals than wild animals, and what was worse, to our own. We stepped up dog training and set to work fixing the gate.

With life slowly returning to some form of normality, we began seeing people from further afield than just the village. El Mexicano popped round to drop us off a local pumpkin as big as Roan, for us to take seed from, and some cherry tomato plants. We planted them up in the veg patch that was proving bountiful despite the draught we were facing. The squashes we'd already got in the ground were growing well, and we harvested red onions aided by fresh garden grown mint tea.

We went to our neighbouring town to visit the cheese lady, who I'd started buying with since pregnant with Roan for she was the only one who had a pasteurised option. She cut Roan off the largest slice of blue cheese which to our surprise he devoured in delight. We bought a punnet of blueberries and then headed to a secret spot along the river, which Jack had first shown us, for a dip. We saw the biggest salmon jumping and hoped that the fisherman upstream didn't get lucky.

And then my parents arrived. We hadn't seen them since mid-March, and it was now mid-July. Roan was so different to when they'd last seen each other, he was now walking! Pulling his weight around Wild Finca; feeding the chickens, ducks and geese, harvesting from the garden (not always the correct veggies, mind you). Fascinated by everything around him, he'd held Stag Beetles and Slow Worms. A little bit too confident at times, the nip from the Woodlouse Spider perhaps a necessary lesson to learn.

My dad arrived first and unsurprisingly there were some tears, with a little person so much changes so quickly and you can't help but feel robbed of the time. It is true that living abroad will always mean that there are longer gaps between time spent together, but when the distance is forced, it is so much harder. There was a lot to catch up on.

As well as showing him all that had changed around Wild Finca, we also went on expeditions a little further afield to a favourite spot in the Picos that Luke and I found in our first year. A spot on the opposite side of the river to El Chorco de los Lobos, where there is a shrine called La Ermita de Corona, which is surrounded by wildflower meadows that stretch for the sky. We took a picnic and sat in the shade of the ash trees, watching Swallowtails, Fritillaries and Skippers floating from flower to flower on their pollen-focussed commutes. Whilst down by the river Purple Emperors puddled, drinking up the minerals from the wet mud. And back home in the evenings, we proudly served him vegetables from the garden, including, in his own words, 'the best carrots I've ever tasted'. It was a purple heritage carrot that had taken some coaxing for him to try in the first instance, his fear of all things vegetable so deeply ingrained. My mum joined a few days after and the joy of reuniting was unceasing.

After my parents left, we continued enjoying our new freedom with more day trips. Another notable one to Riaño, perfectly timed for the hay meadows had just been cut. Getting there was somewhat terrifying; navigating the narrow gorge road and negotiating non-existent passing spots, while huge lorries stacked high with hay bales came hurtling down towards us. However, once there, the wildlife visiting the newly cut lands were abundant. Spotted Flycatchers, Iberian Grey and Red-backed Shrikes hunting from the electricity wires and White Storks in their family groups picking their way through the fields, feasting on the treasures left behind by the harvesters. We don't get White Stork at Wild Finca, but just an hour or so drive away and those fantastically messy nests begin appearing atop pylons and church roofs.

The main species we visited Riaño in search of was the Wild Cat. It was a great place to get almost guaranteed views of the angry looking feline as they hunted voles in the hay meadows. El Mexicano told us once that there were Wild Cats around Wild Finca, and certainly some of the feral cats have some sort of Wild Cat genetics. But amongst the tens of feral cats Olaya fed, and who haunted Wild Finca, we were yet to see a true Wild Cat.

Chapter 26

The Hedges

When lockdown rules completely relaxed, we took a week's birding trip to the pretty village of Quintanilla de Babia, which sits on the edge of the Parque Natural Babia y Luna. It was for the Tourist Board to create some content for Castilla y Leon, and we'd also been tasked with a mission by the Self-Isolating Bird Club to find them a bear.

On our very first walk out of the B&B's front door we were struck by how alive with birdlife the beautifully messy hedgerows were. Endless Red-backed Shrike, Iberian Yellow, White and Grey Wagtails flitted either side of us as we walked down the road. And down at the stream we couldn't get over the number of Nightingales we heard croaking. I even saw my first one (a bit crazy considering I'd made a whole documentary about them!).

We woke early that first morning and headed to a spot twenty minutes from our base called La Peral. A site known for spotting bears. There we met friends who'd driven up for the day, and of the two walking routes out of La Peral we chose the route that went up the hill, not down. buzzards grappled overhead, feeding Common Linnet, and a covey of Red-legged Partridge accompanied our walk. At the view point we'd stopped and scanned the open grassy spots, spotting a large male Wild Cat stalking in one of the fields below. A storm then blew in and we walked back down to a cafe in the village, stopping briefly to talk to some other wildlife watchers along the way. 'Did you see the Wild Cat?' we asked. 'No', they answered, and then asked, 'Did you see the bear and two cubs?'

We risked the second storm to try and get views of said bear, and headed along the second walking route below, but we got caught in an epic hailstorm. We sought cover in a bush until it passed, all the while Roan smiling with glee despite the weather and the lack of bear sightings.

We also visited Lago de Babia where huge flocks of Martins bathed and drank, two Montagu's Harrier patrolled and a large herd of Chamois grazed. For lunch that same day we found a spot just outside Cueta, by the stream, to have our picnic. There butterflies danced atop the Yellow Rattle and Cirl Bunting fed on the seed-heads. A flock of Spotless Starling shook the trees and a little later a pale morph Booted Eagle glided overhead. After we'd eaten, we paddled in the clear waters of the babbling brook whilst Chaffinch flitted along the banks beside us. We spent the afternoon driving the windy roads through the natural park, the roadside fields dotted with Mistle Thrush. And in an open plain a dog fox and vixen hunted, quite content to continue when we pulled over to watch. So much bolder than I'd ever seen our local ones.

During the rest of our stay, we ticked off Northern Wheatear, Cettis Warbler, and the density and variety of birdlife we saw was testament to the area's scrubby edges. We returned home inspired to allow our boundaries even more scope to go wild. A few years ago, when Luke had filmed at Knepp, Charlie Burrell told him that the perfect hedgerow width was fifteen metres. Luke had crawled through one of the Knepp hedgerows to film the cross section. It was made up of a thick thorny scrub all the way through, with larger trees poking out the top and billowing down into wild margins. Perfect nesting and foraging sites, and wildlife highways. And so, along with the ponds, planting up hedgerows had become a second way in which we'd actively started to take more of a role in the transformation of Wild Finca. Dare I say it, it was even possible that these actions were already starting to have an impact for the night we returned from our holiday we sat listening to three croaking Nightingales migrating through, and even spotted one feasting on elderberries. The Red-backed Shrike family were feeding, a Dartford Warbler called, and a Booted Eagle flew overhead. It wasn't quite as wild as where'd we'd just been, but we felt like it was getting there.

Alongside the wonderful wildlife we were witnessing, our veggie patch was also performing so well that we hadn't needed to buy vegetables for the past two months: cucumber, corn, courgette, celery, leeks, beans, aubergine, basil, thyme. We harvested the last of the cherry tomatoes from the plant El Mexicano had brought over. Not a huge haul, for although they'd spread like a creeper way beyond their beds, while doing the garden rounds Roan would often disappear only to be found popping them like sweets.

Towards the end of the summer, we finally went to visit Inacio for some more rabbits. Inacio and his dog lived at the top of the hill in the village, overlooking town. Their barn was the last building along the road that led to the hill's crest. Inacio shook his head and laughed when we explained what had befallen the original pair, and we saw immediately why when he'd opened the barn darn to reveal metal cages, raised from the ground, where his rabbits were kept. The system was simple enough, the poo and pee fell straight through the bars at the bottom, easily swept away from the floor below. And, not only could the rabbits not dig their way out, but the dogs couldn't reach them either. Perhaps not the most enjoyable home for the rabbits, but who were we to judge. Ours may have been freer, but they were also deader. We returned home with four that afternoon, and plans to create something like Inacio's system, but bigger, with more space for the rabbits to roam around. It was Carlos, the Venezuelan, who delivered what we were looking for, salvaged from his new place of work. He'd started working at a Palacio, a large old palace on the other side of the valley and was often offering us bits and bobs the owners were trying to get rid of. This time it was a large metal contraption, essentially three animal cages stacked one on top of the other. With a few holes cut here and there, and a few fashioned ladders allowing them to roam up and down, it was a veritable multi-storey complex for rabbits. We positioned the rabbit palace at the bottom of our stairs, conveniently located to deliver all the veg garden cut-offs the kitchen produced.

With the rabbits now contained, we were having ever more problems with the sheep. It seemed to be the case that just when you had one animal under control, things went wrong with another. With the introduction of the new ewes, the flock was forever escaping and refused to follow Luke when he wanted to move them. The problem was that the new ewes were so feral, not helped by the dog attack, and now Rameses was behaving even wilder than before.

Chapter 27

The Asturcóns

Despite the ongoing unruly sheep situation, for his twenty-ninth birthday, Luke decided to treat himself to two foals. From his reading Luke believed Wild Finca required a broader grazing than what only the sheep could offer. And so, keen to stick with native animals Luke reached out to our old neighbour from the rental, a well-known ganadero of local breeds. By trade our old neighbour was a carpenter, but his true passion was keeping autochthonous species. He had a large flock of Xalda sheep and a small herd of Casina cows, docile Asturian mountain cattle. He also kept Pita Pinta chickens and had been part of the effort of reviving the almost extinct Asturcelta pig. One of our first visits to his finca had been to see one of his Asturcelta sows and her new litter. I managed to stop one of those coming home with us that day, despite Luke's best efforts. They are nevertheless an interesting pig. They are not suited to intensive methods of rearing, and thrive in oak and chestnut forests, which means the meat is always organic and free range. And even though the Asturcelta has a much lower fat content than the more popular breeds of pig, its flavour makes up for it. But, in today's world, it is these qualities that are the reason for the race's near extinction. For quantity over quality is king.

All the carpenter's animals were overseen by three huge Spanish Mastíns. They can be quite a ferocious creature, completely devoted to their charges, and we have had our fair share of run-ins with these dogs in the mountains. I have more fear of mastíns than I do the wolf or bear. But these three were gentle giants, and the puppy of the three was delighted to roll around with Roan while we were there to meet the latest of our old neighbour's animals. Two young Asturcón foals, born in the Sueve mountains to his free-roaming herd.

Jet-black with a long mane, the Asturcón pony was one of the oldest and purest ponies in the world. The first testimony of its existence was recorded in Roman times when the author and naturalist Pliny the Elder, wrote of their unusual gait in his *Naturalis Historia*:

> The Galaicas and Astures tribes of northern Hispania breed a race of horses called CELDONS [in their language]; this small race that [we Romans] call ASTURCÓNES, do not trot but have a special easy step that comes from moving the two legs of each side alternately.

It was here the name Asturcón originated. As well as their unusual gait they were known for their speed and courage in combat. However, they nearly went extinct during the early to mid 1900s, as they were no longer valued for meat or as draft animals, and at their lowest number there were believed to only be forty left. Then, in 1980, conservation efforts began to save this iconic little pony.

The pair were being kept in a field behind our old neighbour's house, and the minute we passed through the gate they galloped to the far end of the pasture. Bottoms against the fence line, they stood shoulder to shoulder as if one animal. They eyed us warily and it'd been impossible to get any closer to them, for they were as wild as the hills they'd been born in. They still had their baby coat, a soft downy brown fluff, this colour apparently an evolutionary defence to camouflage them from predators, no wonder as they were only three months old, and I had my reservations about how young they were. I'd kept horses all my life and knew my way around them pretty confidently, but I'd never kept foals, and these two seemed far too young to be away from their mothers. However, this was the way it was done here, our old neighbour assured us, and he promised that by the end of the week they'd be eating out of our hands. Luke was smitten, to him they were the perfect addition to the Wild Finca dream. So, hands were shaken, and plans were made for them to be dropped off.

During the month of September, we welcomed some incredible migrant birds to Wild Finca. For a few weeks a male goshawk would hang around the chicken coop in the afternoons. It did manage to take out one of our chicks but was disturbed and left it behind, so Luke popped it on the perch the goshawk was frequenting for when it returned. As our friend Will Rose's dad had said, 'a few chickens aren't a bad price to pay to have your own goshawk!' And we agreed. We called it our rent. Then, on the morning of Luke's twenty-ninth birthday, we opened the curtains to find a green sandpiper foraging in the muddy banks of the second, still unlined, pond. To think that this little wading bird would have been breeding up near the Arctic Circle all summer, and was now headed south, and had decided to stop off at our unfinished pond for a pit stop was rather special.

Later that afternoon the ponies were dropped off, and, for the weeks that followed, I became an Asturcón widow.

We named the ponies Pliny and Pear. Pliny after Pliny the Elder, and Pear after our giant pear tree. In preparation of their arrival Luke built a very small paddock, just below the barn, beside the pear. For most hours of the days that followed their arrival, Luke could be found sat quietly with them in the paddock. Pliny and Pear could be found opposite Luke, stood in the same manner as they'd done that very first visit. Bottom to the fence, glued to each other, ears pricked forward in mistrust. If Luke tried to approach them, they would gallop the few metres across the pen, churning up what little grass there was, until very quickly the whole spot became a mud-bath. The treats of bread (a very Asturian method of bribing all farm animals) pony nuts, carrots and apples were point-blank ignored. Only the hay was eaten, and even that would not be approached until we were well clear of the area. It became clear, quite quickly, that a week would not soften their wild hearts, and as much as we valued their free nature, we needed to have some sort of relationship with them. For if they escaped, or were sick or injured, we needed to be able to handle them.

Keeping them penned up for more than ten days was no longer an option, so we tried a new tactic, a tip from El Mexicano's son, to turn them out with a head collar and long rope so that we could catch them easily and handle them daily. This sounded like broken legs and entanglements with trees to me, but with no alternative ideas we gave it a shot. It worked to an extent; we were able to capture them with relative ease. We would then rub them down, talk to them, brush them. But it didn't seem to make much of a difference for the minute we let go of the rope, they kicked their feet in the air and were gone faster than the wind. Then Pear lost her rope within days and, after a particularly scary entanglement with a tree he'd been rubbing against, we soon got rid of Pliny's rope too. I was not particularly happy about all of this. I'd voiced my concerns about getting such young horses, but when Luke has an idea in his head it's near impossible to talk him out of it. So, what was our plan for taming our wild horses? Well, to get another horse of course.

Luke sold it to me this time as something that could pull a cart to help around the farm, and something we could ride. I was keen for Roan to learn to ride as soon as possible and so I agreed to the plan. We originally wanted another Asturcón, to be in keeping with our autochthonous animal theme, but there really was no such thing as a tame Asturcón within our budget. The other problem we found was that all the males were intact, and another stallion was the last thing we wanted. (Pliny was already beginning to prove feisty beyond our capabilities.) And so, we put the word out for any old horse, female or gelded, that was 'noblé' as the Spanish called it (essentially noble, good with people) and could be ridden.

Just as the search for a new horse began, nearly a year to the date, a second duck massacre took place. This time of my own making. I'd prepared a roasted lamb in a salt bake, and whilst it tasted delicious, the whole process called for such a ridiculous amount of salt that for that reason alone, I would never bother again with it. After the cooking process all that could be done with the salt was to bin it. I wish I'd done that, but instead, without thinking, I put it out with the compost. I thought nothing of it until we went to put the ducks to bed that night, only to find five of them dead, one Aylesbury, the rest male Muscovy ducks. They didn't have a scratch on them and although I immediately suspected poisoning, it took me a few days to realise that I had been the perpetrator. After retracing my steps, I remembered that the minute I'd emptied the compost bin the Muscovy's (like usual) had descended, gobbling down every bit of what'd been thrown out. Only the Aylesbury had managed a look-in, the Muscovy's so quick to clear the scraps. I later read that salt in large quantities kills ducks, which is not surprising really. It just never crossed my mind that they would choose to eat it in the first place.

Chapter 28

Mushrooms and Fire Salamanders

With Luke lost to the Asturcón's, I signed Roan and me up to a mushroom walk with Ali. A while back Jack had invited us around for lunch and served us what I initially thought to be chicken curry, which came as a bit of shock as at the time I wasn't eating meat. But it turned out to be a mushroom he'd found in his woodland, a mushroom called Chicken of the Woods, named such for its texture is so like that of actual chicken. After that, I was keen to explore the world of wild mushrooms further and had started observing them during our walks through the woods. I hoped Ali might be able to help me to make the jump from observing to collecting and preparing a mushroom meal for myself.

The walk took place in a beautiful little woodland beside the little village of Corao, known for its biannual cattle markets held as the cows were moved to and from the mountains. There must have been about fifteen of us, all with our wicker baskets. Ali introduced us to Artist's Bracket, a large bracket fungus growing on the side of a fallen oak tree. It was brown on top, with a creamy underside which Ali scratched with a small stick. Where Ali had scratched the marks turned brown and she explained how they could be used to produce artistic images, hence where its common name came from. She showed us an old Beefsteak Fungus on a Sweet Chestnut, another type of bracket fungus, edible if found young enough. There was so many that I found hard to remember, and certainly wouldn't have felt confident identifying myself. The scariest being the Destroying Angel mushroom, which as it's not so subtle name suggests is deadly. It was pure white, and when Ali stopped us to look at it, Roan made a beeline for it. I came away with two hard rules for my new hobby. If it's white, don't touch it. And if there is even the slightest question over its identity, don't eat it. Ali reassured me that with time and exposure I would become more confident, but I did come away from the walk feeling a little overwhelmed by it all.

My first opportunity to try out what I'd learnt from Ali came a few weeks later, when some large tan mushrooms, with a scaly top, creamy gills and a stem that had a mottled brown snakeskin effect, began popping up around the Wild Finca meadows. I was quite sure they were Parasol mushrooms, according to everything I read the snakeskin marked stem was the defining feature, and so I went for it. I cooked them up with some Lea & Perrins and served them with a fried egg. They were delicious! But this idea of picking and eating from outside the vegetable patch seemed to trigger in Roan an insatiable desire to put everything in his mouth. Places to go, animals to see, suspect things to put in my mouth became Roan's life motto. My life was literally all about following in the small but incredibly powerful footsteps of his, all day, every day. And try as I might most days Roan returned home soaked through, dribbling gravel and all manner of other unidentifiable objects, clothes covered in a mixture of chicken poo and mud. A true farm kid.

It was around this time that we heard some rather worrying news, that three parcels of land (two within Wild Finca, and one that surrounded us) had gone on sale. As neighbours we were given first refusal, and two weeks to secure it. It was land we desperately wanted to protect from overgrazing, pesticide/herbicide spraying and potential development, but it was land we simply couldn't afford. We were becoming increasingly aware of a concept known as 'edge effects'. Edge effects were those things that happened around a boundary, they could be positive, neutral or negative, however, in our case, with our neighbour's land management techniques, we were noticing that they were largely negative. From the use of livestock wormers to habitat removal, pesticide use on the orchard above us, to over-grazing, we could only guess of the true extent of the effect they had on Wild Finca and on the wildlife that called it home. The phrase had struck Luke so much that he'd scrawled it on our kitchen whiteboard. To have control of this land would go some way to alleviating some of the negative edge effects, and so we set up a Crowdfund page in the hope that we might be able to raise the funds we needed.

At the same time Luke had taken on a couple of photography shoots for a friend who was actively trying to market some local producers who were making their products in harmony with nature. The first was a local cheese farm in Gamonéu, and Roan and I went along with him for the shoot. On the drive up to the dairy we'd been a little bit disappointed to see several anti-wolf signs in the village, but not surprised given the demonstrations that had taken place there in the past. However, we were happy to meet the owner, who was accepting and adaptive of the wolves that called the same mountains home. He guided us around his dairy, introduced us to his sheep and cows, and then took us to the cave where his cheese was aged. We spoke about the possibility of labelling his product as 'wolf friendly' but he said it would cause too many personal problems with his neighbour. We went home with a lot to consider, and a wheel of cheese in exchange for the photos.

The second shoot was with a beekeeper. The friend who'd asked Luke along to this and to photograph the cheesemaker, intended to create an online shop for the beekeeper and cheesemaker to sell their products. He aimed to market them not only as organic but also wolf and bear friendly. We were very excited by the concept and wanted to support the idea as best we could. With the community we'd built up via the Self-Isolating Bird Club, we knew we had an audience that would be interested in this sort of produce.

Meanwhile, our own beekeeping experience had come to an end. At the end of the swarm season, we'd collected the hive from the Snake Pit promptly, but we were a bit lackadaisical about removing the one on Los Pinos. The brambles had grown so much we needed a machete to access it, so it had gone on the to-do list where it kept being knocked further and further down by weather and injury (Luke had done his back in digging ponds, and a good glut of rain in the first week of November had put all outdoor jobs on hold).

With the lack of success, we had made the decision to put our three boxes, two supers (the boxes that go on top for collecting the honey), full sets of racks and two anti-Asian Hornet boxes up for sale. With two interested buyers Luke braved the now dwindling, but still chilly, rain to collect the final beehive. I was working in the house when I had received his message: 'the hive is active!' I raced down to the pines and arrived as two bees flew into the beehive. One hand on the metal lid gave no doubt that it was indeed active, the warmth radiating upwards generated by the busy little bodies within. We were both astonished. We traced back to the last time we had checked the hive and agreed that the swarm must have moved in sometime the previous month, which had been unseasonably warm.

Not long after I had arrived so had our nemesis, the Asian Hornet. It had entered the hive and reappeared a few moments later with a victim. Luke quickly ran back up to the barn to get one of the anti-Asian Hornet boxes to attach to the entrance. While Luke was fitting the box he had been able to kill the Asian Hornet, but there would undoubtedly be more. Just the month before we had seen dozens of them fretting our ivy bushes. To truly destroy an Asian Hornet population, you must target them at their source, and apart from one nest we had spotted across the valley, which had now been dealt with, and a second in our neighbour's orchard, which had also been destroyed, we had no idea where the new nest was. Any other forms of capturing the Asian Hornet were too indiscriminate, and often laid siege to a far greater percentage of other types of bees, wasps and flies. So, we put our faith in the anti-Asian Hornet box for now, in the hope that it would give the bees a fighting chance by stopping the hornets from at least entering the hive. It was too cold that day to open up the hive and check the health of the swarm, but we did hazard a guess that they would need feeding over winter if they were to survive, for it was unlikely they would have time to build up stores for the winter.

The opportunity to check the hive did not come until the following month, for that November turned into a month of relentless rain. Greater than 40mm fell each day for three weeks solid, and unfortunately the beehive had not survived. Between the Asian Hornets and the rain, they hadn't stood a chance, and on opening the box we found the racks completely empty. We took down the final box, stacked it alongside the other in our hórreo and decided to have a break from our never-ending bee bad luck.

One warm wet evening we were in town for drinks that were turning into dinner, which meant Luke needed to nip home to put the chickens, ducks and geese to bed. Where the road straightens up to the fuente, Luke spotted his first Fire Salamander. He slammed on the brakes and excitedly jumped out to get photo evidence. But he needn't have worried about missing it for they were all the way along the road to Wild Finca, with most requiring a little assistance clearing the road. Luke returned to the pub beyond ecstatic. He'd finally seen his first Fire Salamander. Fire Salamanders had been a fascination for Luke for as long as he could remember. Evidence of this enchantment recently re-discovered by his father when he'd been going through Luke's old schoolbooks, an impressively realistic depiction signed by Luke Massey, aged six years old. And now he owned a farm with resident Fire Salamanders. For the nights that followed they were out in force, and on one night we counted over forty.

The rain lasted the whole of the month, and we made the most of it by cutting Goat Willow at Ali's and planting them along the boundaries at Wild Finca. The hedges we'd been nurturing were slowly getting thicker, the pioneering brambles (much maligned by our neighbours) protecting trees that were now beginning to emerge above the tangle of them. And as we worked on the land and shared our endeavours online the Crowdfund for the neighbour's land ticked up. We watched with disbelief as each donation added up and we reached our target. Five hundred and fifty-seven people donated so that we could become the custodians of the land, an astonishing amount of faith. Through sharing what we were up to with the Self Isolating Bird Club, and on various other social media channels, the vision of Wild Finca had clearly resonated with people. What an incredible amount of trust these people had now put in us. We went up to the top plot that evening to celebrate and to meditate on the future of Wild Finca. The plot had not been touched for a while, the owners not having use for it, and it was already a fantastic mosaic of habitat. The boundary of the land was made up of a dense wall of gorse, whilst below lay a meadow full of Wild Fennel. Perhaps the gorse might need a bit of tending to, and to ensure the meadow stayed such some light grazing would be needed. But for now, we felt justified in continuing as we were, trial and error and seeking out advice from people who knew what they were doing. We now had financial backers, who by their actions had proven they believed in us and our vision. It was an astonishing feeling to have such support.

Chapter 29

A New Year's Walk

Storms defined the end of the year. Storm Belle lasted a weekend, rolled in with 90km/h winds and deposited 120mm of rain. Luke worked hard at securing Wild Finca, but our lemon trees took a battering, a few gates were splintered from their hinges, a pile of plant pots overlooked in the clean-up had reached all corners of the land and Old Mamma ended up at the centre of a bramble bush. Whether she had got there of her own accord, for protection, or had been put there by Belle we would never know. Having called herself hoarse to be found, she'd gone straight back to grazing on her release, seemingly none the worse for it.

Despite the changeable weather there had been hunts across the land since the first day of the season and they'd continued every Thursday, and sometimes both days of the weekend. Having not been able to make the most of their 'essential workers' status over the pandemic, they sure were making up for it this season.

Around Christmas time we faced the largest hunt we'd seen so far. There must have been twenty or so men in high-vis jackets, with more dogs howling than I could see, all coming over the brow of the hill above us, and heading, what felt like, straight for the house. Two of the dogs got in with Pliny and Pear, who'd been grazing calmly in our highest fields but were now galloping around manically. The whole structure was different today. Normally the hunts started at the other end of the valley, driving through the woods below us. While some men would come from the footpath, across our land and enter the woods, inevitably it always ended up that the guns were below us.

But today it wasn't happening below us, instead it surrounded us. And then five or so men with guns appeared on the footpath, converging on the gate we'd put in. One opened the gate and came through, a second followed, while the rest spread themselves along the green route. I was beside myself by this point, and begged Luke to go and find out what their plan was. Above us was common land, we had no right to tell them what they could and couldn't do there. But they were now on our land, with guns. Luke took Otis and went to confront them. I watched through binoculars as Luke and Otis approached the gunman and a conversation began. After five minutes the gunman retreated, and Luke returned. I met him at the door, anxious to find out what had happened. Luke had asked what the plan was, and they had replied that it was to drive the boar onto our land and shoot it there, for our land was flat and conveniently located. When Luke explained that it was private land, that we had sheep here, that we hoped to walk our fields with our young son and three dogs that day and that we didn't want wildlife being killed here, they'd agreed to re-route the hunt through the common land. They may have used stronger language away from us, for their new route was a much tougher landscape to navigate, but they'd remained polite and obliging once faced with Luke's reasoning.

It was one of my biggest stresses living at Wild Finca. The sound of the dogs and the sight of men in high-vis jackets on our boundaries, oftentimes destined for our land. Even worse when you could hear them but couldn't see them. To walk anywhere during hunting season, it was advised we too wore high-visibility jackets: walks through the woods, must wear high-vis; taking the dogs for a walk, don't forget the high-vis; checking the horses' water, high-vis needed; and counting the sheep, don't do it without high-vis. Why? Because stories of accidental shootings were rife. The lady hanging her laundry, more recently a man bent over picking mushrooms mistaken for a Wild Boar. I did not fear wolves, I did not fear bears, it was the hunters I was afraid of.

The first year we moved in they had been regular, once a week, if we were lucky every two weeks, and that had felt too much. This year was worse, and it was starting to really get to us both. The yowling dogs felt relentless, and the high-vis jackets and loaded guns, slung haphazardly over shoulders, spotted almost daily. Tourism Asturias calls Asturias 'a true hunting paradise', and boy were they making the most of it.

On another occasion an old Woodcock hunter had come through our gate at the bottom of Wild Finca where our boundary meets the woods. He had with him three spaniels, free roaming, and a loaded gun nonchalantly slung over his shoulder. Otis had alerted Luke to them and the pair had gone down to see what was going on. On approaching, the man had unloaded his gun and, looking very surprised at being confronted, made no secret that he thought the land was abandoned. Our wilder ways of managing had led him to believe that entry was fair game. He claimed he never intended to hunt the land but was merely passing through, which we have been led to believe is completely legal.

I hated it all. And, after finding yet another group of hunters with dogs off the lead on our land, Luke and I hit our stress threshold. This was no way to live, in fear from September through to March. Perhaps Wild Finca wasn't our forever home. In that moment we remembered Jack, who'd just sold his property, not dissimilar to ours, to a young family, but who'd also had a couple of Dutch guys interested. We'd messaged Jack for their number and reached out. The Dutch had replied almost immediately, keen for a viewing. We even organised a time for them to come and visit, but the next morning we called off the meeting. People believed in us; they'd just helped us secure more land to protect. And apart from that, where else would we go? Certainly not back to the UK. Asturias had our hearts.

And whilst the hunting situation at times felt unbearable, the rest of our home was pretty damned near perfect. Instead, we vowed to work harder at removing hunting access and in the meantime, for our sanity, at the sight or sound of a hunt, after securing the animals, we'd taken to escaping the farm. The next hunt happened to be New Year's Day, and pre-empting their imminent arrival (all of the Christmas festive period was celebrated with a hunt) we'd headed out, only ten minutes up the road, but somewhere we were sure there'd be no hunters.

The walk began with an incline between tall pine trees. Their needles and the little bit of slush that remained from the first snow was springy underfoot. A flock of Crested Tits flitted through the canopy overhead.

At the crest we stepped up and over a natural rocky staircase and followed the trail that winds its way across the side of the mountain. The slush was thicker there, browner from frequent footfall. In the heather above horses grazed, some Asturcóns, and a few Pottokas, another ancient breed from the Cantabria region. Both hardy creatures, well adapted to the, at times, inhospitable mountainsides.

A man with a snowboard strapped to his back strode past us, his destination the enormous iron cross that marks the summit of Picu Pienzu. But we were happy pottering along the lower crest for our destination was not so far. We stopped a few times to let Roan run around. It was only the second time he'd seen snow, the first was at the beginning of the month when it'd fallen at home, a very rare occurrence Olaya told us. The snow had lasted barely a day before the temperate climate returned the magically transformed landscape that same afternoon. The ducks pronounced footprints, within which Roan had joyfully placed his own little feet, melting within hours of appearing.

Reaching about 1000m, at the heart of the Sueve range and across the valley to our right we saw the forest of La Biescona, a beautiful beech wood. They say in ten years the Cantabrian

Brown Bear may have reached here. Perhaps, if there is enough food and the ever-marching eucalyptus plantations are defeated. At our back stretched the Bay of Biscay, and ahead of us towered the Picos de Europa. The 'peaks of Europe', named such by sailors returning from the Americas, for it was the first land seen. They are magnificent and at their prime spots they are the perfect example of an Atlantic ecosystem, packed with oak and beech groves, and wildlife, extraordinary wildlife that'd been our calling to the area.

The snow became thicker, more virgin, as our route diverged from the well-trodden path across the now hidden green pastures of Bustaco. Our going slowed and on my back Roan was now fast asleep. Luke stopped a little further ahead, the snow encasing his calves. Breathing heavily, I joined him, and he handed me the binoculars. The hunt had finished, no orange jackets or loose dogs to be seen. Just our home, perhaps two miles as the Griffon Vulture flew. From this height she looked glorious. There was no way we were going to be forced from Wild Finca.

Chapter 30

Notes from Wild Finca

January was a month for ponds. Luke spent the first week hard at work on the second large pond, the one in the meadow below the barn, levelling out the edges for smaller, shallower ponds that were bird and baby friendly. Ro had fallen in the first pond a few times whilst exploring, the one below the pear tree, never alone of course, but it had reinforced why the edges needed to be shallower, making that job a priority. Once happy with his remodelling Luke then lined it, this time just in time for the two days' solid rain which filled the pond nicely. Next, he'd headed down to alongside Los Pinos and began working on another new pond there.

We also started the year filming a new series called *Notes from Wild Finca*. It was a sort of diary of the goings on of both our life and the wildlife. What the successful Crowdfunder had shown us was that people were enjoying following Wild Finca and, sort of as a thank you, but also as a way of sharing ideas of how to make wildlife welcome, we set ourselves the New Year's resolution of releasing a film a month. It meant that Luke now went most places with a camera, and he captured some amazing wildlife behaviour: a Golden Eagle alighting on the eucalyptus and being mobbed by a Carrion Crow and a Eurasian Magpie; the Wild Narcissus blooming out of seemingly nowhere along one of the routes we regularly walked; and then, while working on his new pond, he'd heard from the other side of the scrub one of our Xalda's baa'ing softly. He popped his head over and found Old Mamma with a new lamb. It was another boy, and she did as she had done before, keeping him hidden away until he was strong enough to join the flock. Unfortunately, the lambs that followed were not so doted upon. The second arrival, another male, and the third, a female, had to be brought into the barn for a few days with their mothers, due to their mothers trying to keep up with the flock from the moment their lambs hit the ground. But it was our final lamb, a little female, who really put us through our novice sheep-keeping paces.

Like the two before, the lamb was on the move with the flock from the moment she arrived. All three born to first-time mothers, whose lack of experience had been obvious. However, she appeared stronger than the other two, so we made the decision to leave her to it. But, halfway through our evening drinks on the mound, we heard the Common Ravens begin to cronk. And then they swooped down towards the forest, where we knew the sheep had taken to settling for the night. Without saying a word Luke dropped his bottle and sprinted towards them, and five minutes later he returned with the sorriest looking creature. A bundle of black fluff and bones that weighed barely enough to register in your arms.

He'd found the lamb with three ravens on top of her and Mum nowhere to be seen. The mother hadn't even approached when Luke went to pick up the lamb. At first glance the lamb looked to have fared alright from the encounter. She was not blind, and she still had her tongue, which was a relief for this was where ravens will target. There was only one small cut that we could see. Our instinct was to get her reunited with her mother as soon as possible, so while Roan and I sat with the lamb, Luke went to catch Mum. He returned an hour or so later and we reunited the pair in the barn. Luke latched the lamb to the ewe's teat, and it tried to feed, but as soon as Luke let go the little lamb collapsed. We put it down to exhaustion and thought it best to leave the pair alone for the night, to settle and hopefully bond. By the next morning it was obvious that Mum had no interest in the lamb, and as we approached them, she'd trampled the lamb that was now too weak to stand.

We released the mother, took the lamb up to the house and Luke popped to town for milk replacer. She didn't feed well so we syringed the milk down her throat over those early days, and it must have been on about day three, after she still couldn't stand, that we finally located the real problem. The ravens had sliced her open from her chin all the way down her tummy to her tail, and in places the wound had gone to the bone. We originally missed it for the flap of skin had reattached in sections. Thanks to Instagram we'd recently begun following a lady called Rebecca Hosking who kept a flock of sheep in Devon, which she called 'the Forever Flock,' and we'd reached out to her for advice on what to do with our new orphaned lamb. Rebecca kindly replied and, on her advice, along with the honey we'd been using to treat the wound, we picked up some silver veterinary spray. Despite our efforts the little lamb didn't appear to be getting any stronger. She still wasn't feeding, and the likelihood of infection, despite our treatment, was high. Then suddenly, she rallied, and from there she went from strength to strength. We named her Blanca due to her white head on her otherwise black body.

At the same time as Blanca's arrival, we'd been fostering three puppies for a local rescue. And of course, fostering for one had turned into adoption. He was so small he fitted in my pocket, making him the smallest animal on the farm, and probably not the most sensible farm addition. We named him Atlas Bumblebee, a big name for a small dog. Luke and I had gone with Atlas but then Ro had learnt the word bumblebee and had started calling him Bumba. When she was strong enough, Blanca had moved under the hórreo with Bumba and his siblings.

It wasn't just reviving orphaned lambs that we turned to Rebecca for. It was also Rebecca's farming theory, called 'Agriwilding', that we connected with, and we began to take real inspiration from her work for our developing vision for Wild

Finca. We had arrived at Wild Finca with a vision of 'rewilding', riding the wave that this was the key to ecological restoration; by leaving the land completely to its own devices. However, we wanted to also live from the land ourselves. On top of that we were learning that if we did just leave everything to its own accord, the land would likely all return to woodland, and there were many species here that did not live in woodland (Red-backed Shrikes being one of them). And so, the longer we lived at Wild Finca, the more we realised that perhaps rewilding wasn't the correct term for what we were doing. For instinctually we had begun to move towards something else, and it was Rebecca who put this 'something else' into words for us.

With Rebecca's help we began to build further on our belief that domesticated animals such as sheep, horses and cows could, if managed correctly, be a force of good for a balanced ecosystem. And what Rebecca's teachings reminded us of was that humans were not separate from nature. More than that, humans were as much a keystone species as the wolves, beavers and eagles that were the pinnacle of the rewilding movement. So, to remove ourselves from the picture, to separate land for wildlife from land for us, was the completely wrong way of looking at it.

As Rebecca said, 'Of all the species on this planet, [humans] have demonstrated the ability to profoundly change ecosystems, but unlike other species we can and do change habitats to the detriment of all others. The key is realising we have a choice.' And so, our aims for Wild Finca began to align more with the principles for agriwilding. Below are the principles Rebecca and her friend Tim Green attributed to the term:

1. View your farm as an ecosystem – make it a part of your working day to stop, observe and continually learn its ways. Understand this can't be done in weeks or even years. It's a lifetime of continual learning.

2. Regard and address all species as equal cohabitants – they all have value.

3. Never view any species as immediately unwelcome – instead understand they all have a message for you to learn.

4. Enable domestic and wild species to fully intertwine within the ecological web of the land base.

5. Allow other cohabitants the space and peace they require. Remember their needs to life are as pressing as ours.

6. Take time to fully understand your own agency within your ecological land base.

7. Understand the roles of keystone species and work hard to act as one.

8. Finally, never sacrifice and destroy ecological wealth for financial gain. When money is tight, always find another way.

These principles moved us away from the idea of rewilding for most of the land at Wild Finca, towards a more holistic, inclusive existence which considered us as part of the ecosystem. It was not a case of us dismissing rewilding entirely, we understood, for example, how rewilding unproductive land could restore water tables, prevent flooding, provide habitat for pollinating insects and act as natural pest controls. As Knepp put it, 'rewilding can act as the webbing running through our farmed landscapes, providing the life support system, increasing natural resilience and acting as a buffer against increasingly frequent extreme weather events.'

However, our main focusses at Wild Finca had always been two-fold: the wildlife and sustainable living for our family. We concluded that agriwilding with a touch of rewilding was the composition best suited to us.

Chapter 31

Agriwilding in Practice

We'd spent the past two hours searching frantically for our escaped ponies. Although pony nuts were helping, the Asturcóns would now eat out of hand, we were no closer to getting a head collar on them let alone being able to lead them anywhere. As it turned out Pliny and Pear hadn't strayed far and were still on our land, albeit in a different field to the one they ought to have been in. But their companion, Kalahari, a friendly but feisty stallion lent by El Mexicano's son, was still nowhere to be found. This decided it, if we ever found him, Kalahari would be the final offering in the long line of horses El Mexicano's son had sent to try and help habituate the Asturcóns, but who'd turned out to be harder work than Pliny and Pear. The horses El Mexicano's son lent us on rotation were either younger than our two and/or a bit crazy. And although the Asturcóns had become tamer, there was still a long way to go, and being responsible for someone else's lively horses was proving more work than it was worth. Fortunately for us the nephew with the horses, whilst checking his own, had spotted Kalahari on his way into town. Whether on the tail of a mare in heat, or trying to find his way home, who was to know, but he'd tied Kalahari to the nearest tree and called us. Having watched from afar the string of loony horses we'd hosted, the nephew's parting words were that if we were still looking, he knew of just the horse for us.

A Hispano-Bretón, twelve years old, that lived (and the nephew gestured to us) across that valley and over the mountain. The Hispano-Bretón was a horse bred by crossing the Spanish horse with the Bretón horse from France, to fulfil the agricultural needs of the mountainous areas. So at least we could be sure it was well adapted to the landscape. We headed over one sunny

March day to meet Chula. Brown, with a black mane, tail and socks, a white flash on her forehead and a greying muzzle, she was a monster of a horse. Strong as an ox but as gentle as a lamb. Since hearing about her the horse had aged somewhat, seventeen was what her passport said (and a vet later guessed she was closer to twenty) so she was a fair bit older than I'd hoped for, but she fitted the brief, and the budget. Plus, Roan was besotted with her and smothered her with sloppy kisses which she accepted graciously. I walked her the two hours back home the following day. Apparently, she'd been born in our little village, and she certainly strode into Wild Finca as if she owned the place. We introduced her to Pliny and Pear the following morning, who looked like toys in comparison, and while Chula was as cool as a cucumber at the introductions, the babies huffed and puffed in their excitement.

With the active role we'd been taking within Wild Finca now justified by Rebecca, the to-do list grew exponentially. One of the habitats which we'd been in two minds about leaving to its own devices was the gorse. Specifically, a patch at the top of our land that borders the footpath, where large swathes untended by man or beast had started to become both a hazard, and unproductive for wildlife. We began researching gorse and its role within the environment and read that bushes and stands of gorse start to lose their ecological value after approximately ten years, for they become leggy and die-off occurs. Without the compact spiky structure many birds and mammals ceased to use them as nesting sites, and at the same time the gorse became a fire hazard. With a fair swathe of gorse located on our boundaries, if the neighbouring land was to burn then these gorse stands could end up channelling the flames directly onto Wild Finca.

Not long after we'd bought Wild Finca a fire had burned out of control and crept to the very boundary of our new home. We were away at the time, but Ali had kept checking on the farm for us, and we spent two very nervous days following its progress. At one point it looked highly likely Wild Finca would be a wasteland by the time we got back. That has been our closest call to date, but we anticipate it will happen again for the farmer who does it is well known locally, and we have been outright warned by neighbours of the threat. The 'Mala Gana' (the 'bad farmer' they call him) does not have enough grazing for his animals and so he depends on the common lands, and burns them to regenerate grass, to feed his livestock. Gorse is highly flammable and many a fire is set by local farmers in these parts to clear large areas of it. A not particularly considered method of clearing, for fire encourages the germination of gorse.

And it's not just Mala Gana, there'd been many fires down the valley since we'd first moved in. These fires tended to be set at all times of the year at the end of long dry spells on tinder-box dry days when rain is forecast for the days after the fires are set. But the smoke still haunts you for the duration of the fires, and if the rain doesn't come when it's due, well, let's just say we spend those days sick with fear watching the fire consume the landscape, edging closer and closer. The hydroplanes and helicopters criss-crossing the skies from fire to river and back again, their hauls barely making a dent on the fires they're dumped on. Floating embers, blown in from across the valley, dancing across our crackling dry grasses, closer and closer to our home, threatening to alight the beds we sleep in, the barns our animals are kept in. And so, Luke had started to cut fire breaks on our boundaries.

But with careful management, gorse's value for wildlife could also be maintained. Compact gorse is ideal for a range of nesting birds and its dense structure provides important refuge for birds in harsh weather. Plus, it's an incredibly important source for pollinators, for gorse has a long flowering period making it a significant nectar source when little else is in flower, as well as a yummy snack for us.

So, to resurrect our gorse Luke channelled his inner bison/ auroch/straight-tusked elephant. He would cut back the oldest and leggiest bits, chopping them to ground level and removing them to make dead hedges elsewhere. In some areas, especially where we'd seen orchids and wild iris, he cleared to create open areas for the flowers to thrive. And the cleared gorse didn't go to waste. With some old posts from a boundary line, some coppiced hazel and the cut gorse, he created 'dead hedges', to provide overwintering and breeding habitat for all manner of birds, beetles and reptiles. They also acted as natural fences for the sheep and horses, allowing the orchids and irises to bloom without grazing pressure. Another dead hedge was laid alongside some willow saplings, in the hope that by next spring the area would be buzzing with life. Old gorse entwined with living willow and hazel.

The chopping, splintering and squashing of the old growth was all done at a time when it would have the smallest impact on Wild Finca's wildlife, and even though the weather remained chilly, within weeks the cut-back gorse began to sprout bright green new shoots.

Luke would return from his gorse wrangling covered head to toe in spikes, sneaking his clothing into the washing so that we all got to enjoy the feeling of thorns in our pants for weeks to come. Natural acupuncture, he joked.

And not all the gorse was cut back, for the plan was to let certain areas succumb to natural succession, particularly around the edges of the forest, our rewilding spots. A traditional old English forester's saying is that 'the thorn is the mother of the oak', and a Danish expression for thorny scrub is 'skovens vugge' meaning 'the forest's cradle'. In these two proverbs they are talking more about blackthorn and hawthorn, but gorse and bramble (two things we have in abundance at Wild Finca) are also pioneer species, and if you go into the forest, you can see examples of where they have played this role. There you'll find remnant patches of gorse and brambles from natural succession of years gone by, their job now done, as they die back in the shade of the new forest.

Fencing was another high priority job that never seemed to end. While Chula was doing as hoped and teaching the Asturcóns that we were to be trusted, Chula's own love for humans was fence-defying. No matter how fresh the pasture, she was always looking for an escape route to get closer to us. Within the first week she destroyed a brand-new fence and, after endless repairs which she would then bash through as if the chestnut posts were nothing more than twigs, we reluctantly resigned ourselves to the fact that the only way to keep Chula where we wanted her was with electric fencing. Luke joked that we really *were* a rewilding project, now that we had our very own bison.

In the beginning of our time at Wild Finca we'd allowed the sheep to free roam and, to an extent, when the horses arrived, they too had been allowed larger areas to graze as and when they wished. The only real moves were across the footpath to land that wasn't connected to the main block at Wild Finca. As we'd neared completion of fencing the boundary of Wild Finca, we began to question if an open format on the rest of the land was truly right for us. We were finding that the sheep and horses were not moving around the land, instead they would find spots they liked the most, the freshest grasses or the comfiest sheltered spots and hang out there until the grazing was finished and they were forced to move elsewhere. And so, we'd begun work on some dividing fences, however, these dividing fencing turned out to be a rash decision, for after living within the landscape through a full set of seasons we'd started to feel that they weren't in the right place. Fortunately, we hadn't done too many, mainly due to the cost of the chestnut posts.

Rebecca recommended that to begin with we should use electric fencing, as these could be adapted as we went. And so, we sat down one evening and divided the land into as similar sized portions as was possible, guesstimating the number of days each should be grazed (between two to five days per location). For the weeks following, we spent the days setting up a ridiculous amount of electric fencing across Wild Finca.

It didn't start too well. To save on time we only went for two strands of electric wire. The sheep quickly learnt that they could easily squeeze below the bottom strand, the electric a mere fly on their thick wool coats. As a quick fix we moved the two strands down, but then the horses realised how easy it was to jump so that didn't work either. In the end we gave in and added a third strand, but then another problem arose. We'd been keeping the sheep and the horses together, like the antelope and the warthogs of the African plains, but the horses, mainly Pliny and Pear, were quite aggressive to the sheep. Chasing them, oftentimes full speed, into the electric fencing. One afternoon we spotted Pliny kneeling on one of the sheep. Luke went running and shouting down to the field to get him to release the poor shocked sheep, which escaped leaving tufts of wool in its wake. We separated them and adapted the grazing rotation accordingly.

Chapter 32

The Worm Moon

The Swallows arrived the day before the Worm Moon, as Olaya called it. I'd had to google how this full moon got its name, and the most common origin was that it came from native North American tribes, who named it so because it appeared at the same time as the ground began to thaw and the Earthworms emerged. Essentially, the Worm Moon marked the end of winter and the start of spring, as the very first signs of life began to wake from their winter dormancy.

We welcomed the Worm Moon after another cold and windy winter. At least the new roof Luke had fitted towards the end of the summer had taken the edge off the drastic plunges in degrees (both ways) inside the house. He'd ended up fitting an insulation and panel combination specifically designed for covering old asbestos roofing, and he'd done an amazing job, not least because when the windstorms hit it hadn't felt like the roof was being ripped from above us as we lay in bed. But there was still work to be done, for although the heat was no longer being lost overhead, it was still being lost through the floor. And so, the next job before the following winter was to insulate the ceiling of the barn below.

Home improvements weren't limited to just us. We spent the beginning of the month of March making and putting up bird boxes. Eight in total: two Redstart boxes, three tit boxes, three open fronted boxes that would hopefully work for a selection of species (Robin, Flycatcher, Wren). The gorse bushes started to bush out, creating thick dense pockets, which would hopefully fit the requirements of small birds, like Dartford Warblers, to nest in.

We also wrapped up our tree planting for the season. There is an art to tree planting, for it must be done when the plants are dormant, and the weather and soil conditions are optimum. This ensures they can establish roots before they are exposed to stressors, such as high heat, low temperatures, or not enough water, which makes late autumn, through the winter months and up to the beginning of spring the best time to plant trees. This year we'd found the best month to be February, and we'd spend our afternoons digging up saplings from spots where they would never see full growth and relocating them to spots where their chances were better. Like the Mediterranean Buckthorn, Silver Birch and Common Hazel we'd taken up from around the old barn that was next on the list for renovation. Luke and Roan went over to the southern block, to the plot that is already being taken back by the forest below, and where Common Hazel, Silver Birch, English Oak and Common Holly range from seedlings to five years old. It's an incredibly dense area of young trees, where most won't survive due to crowding, and so they thinned them out and added all those harvested to the hedge line Luke was creating between our bottom fields. Interspersed with a few fruit trees we bought in, the plan is to build wildlife corridors across Wild Finca that connect with the forest.

Our active building of hedgerows and planting of trees baffled our neighbours. Both the nephews chuckled openly at Luke as they found him, yet again, bent double, spade in hand, putting more saplings along a boundary. Inspired by our trips elsewhere, it had always confused us why Wild Finca didn't have hedgerows, for you could tell hedgerows existed in the past at Wild Finca and its surrounds. But somewhere along the way they'd been replaced with barbed wire fences. Since building our own hedgerows back up we were finding that our neighbours' animals were gravitating to our boundaries and munching on the hedgerows that we were allowing to grow wild. We have been told that cows eat grass and grass only, but our neighbours' cows' choices suggest otherwise. And our own animals are often observed eating all sorts of different forage. Horses have been found to eat more than twenty-six plant species a day given the opportunity, but the most exciting realisation for us was when we first watched them nibbling the new shoots of the gorse Luke had bashed back.

And yet we were still regularly observing hedgerows being actively stripped out from around us. The mindset was that if it wasn't good for grazing or growing maize, then it was no good. Ramiro, who owned the plot in the middle of Wild Finca, also owned another beautiful spot the other side of Olaya's. A sloped meadow, about a hectare in size, interspersed with a giant cherry and five delicious apple trees. Luke once told him how much he liked the plot and how we envied his trees, for we started off with very few trees in our fields at Wild Finca. Ramiro replied that having fewer trees was much better, and he said that if he'd the money he'd pay for someone to chop them down. Luke suggested that perhaps the trees were good for shelter/food/scratching, but Ramiro had rolled his eyes. What do animals need shelter for anyway?

Work in the vegetable patch was full steam ahead, with the 'help' of Roan, Blanca and Bumba. While Blanca and Bumba napped in the straw that'd been laid to suppress weeds and keep the soil warm, Roan would follow behind Luke and pull out anything he planted, until he got distracted by something else – worms and Midwife Toads being his favourite things to play with. Midwife Toads, recognisable by their distinctive call which sounds like an electronic beeping, were often found burrowed in the soil and a few times Roan spotted a male with eggs wrapped around its hind legs, en route to find a suitable pond to deposit in. Two rhubarb crowns that had come from my grandad's garden in the UK had taken, and we harvested purple sprouting broccoli and Romanesco from the garden for dinner.

With the hunting season over, we returned to spending time in the woods foraging for Primroses whilst keeping an eye out for Red Squirrels. Catching sight of that distinctive rusty coloured fur flitting between the branches, those characteristic little ear tufts, was always so exciting. On another trip we spotted a Black Woodpecker, the largest woodpecker in Europe, that we'd heard calling many times before but had otherwise so far proved elusive. Another beautiful afternoon was spent down by the stream, beneath the dappled sunlight collecting Wild Garlic. We welcomed back the Swifts, screaming and whirling overhead. The Chiffchaffs also now returned, and the Early Purple Orchids too, which had become synonymous with Wild Finca for us, after them welcoming us along the drive that very first time we'd visited.

Then, one morning, I heard heavy stomping boots on the stairs and the door swung open. 'It's a singing Nightingale! Quick!' Luke shouted. I'd barely time to throw Luke the video camera so that he could capture it for *Notes from Wild Finca* before he was back down the stairs. We'd been in the midst of rushing out the door for a day sorting Roan's residency in the city. It had taken months to get this first appointment and I'd been mid-wrestling Roan into clothing while Luke was rushing to do the animal rounds. But Daddy's excited voice made Roan a bit more compliant, his shoes went on more easily and we were out of the door in hot pursuit.

That undeniable sound of a Nightingale trilling could be heard from the moment we stepped foot outside the front door. With Roan in tow, I headed off in the direction I thought the song was coming from: down the back passageway, up the green route via the fuente, back down the driveway and then I spotted Luke crossing the far field. Because Wild Finca sits in a sort of bowl, I often mis-locate birdcalls as they echo around and had clearly done so again. We met at the gateway by the chicken coop, the singing now ceased, and now late for Roan's residency meeting we called off the hunt and headed for the city. (We fortunately made the appointment, and Roan's residency application was approved.)

Although we'd had Nightingale passing through on migration the previous autumn, in our time at Wild Finca we had never had a singing one in spring. And this meant, potentially, a male looking to set up territory.

Luke had first heard it in a scrubby patch just off our land, but there was no water there and we hoped Luke's pond obsession might entice it over to our side, where he'd only recently completed pond number six. When we'd bought Wild Finca it had no year-round standing water, and in the time since moving in Luke had not only built the two large ponds by the house, but an additional four smaller ponds, expressly for the wildlife. It had become a bit of a running joke in our household, his obsession with pond building. If I couldn't find Luke, and I knew he wasn't necessarily doing something that I classified as important, I would most likely find him digging a new pond or working on an older one. Ponds, it seems, are never truly finished. In fact, his pond obsession probably became the thing we argued most about. In the unlikely event that you feel you are on top of things at a place like Wild Finca, there is always maintenance to be done, so really, there was no such thing as a job completed. However, the prioritisation of 'to-dos' was often quite different for Luke and me. Whilst ponds did not feature high up on my list, not even top twenty, they never moved from Luke's top five.

There was no singing that evening, but it was cold and windy so not too surprising. The next morning Luke headed out early and we received a message that he'd found two singing Nightingales at the bottom of our hill, just above the woods. We made up a flask of coffee, grabbed the picnic rug, wrapped up warm for a chilly mist still hung in the valley, and headed down to join him and enjoy a morning serenade by our visitors. The dogs and Blanca came along too. We'd set up in the dewy grass, on the knoll of the hill that precedes the sharp drop down to the forest and, amongst the usual dawn chorus of Blackbird, Robin and Wren there was the unique addition of two Nightingales. It was heavenly. When the singing ended, we returned to the house via the ponds, secretly hoping the Nightingales were watching and would find them sufficient for their needs. Sadly, they did not, and after three more mornings' singing, the Nightingales moved on.

Chapter 33

Playing the Wolf

While the first pond below the giant pear was flourishing, the second pond was turning into a war of attrition. After being lined the first time the rains had filled it nicely, but as quickly as it had filled it had then emptied. On inspection Luke found three holes: two he put down to the dogs (who loved to do their zoomies around the edge) and the third, at the base, the result of a sharp stone he'd missed whilst clearing. Luke took advantage of the rips, removed the entire liner and spent days reshaping the pond, adding new banks, an island, and even additional side ponds, before re-laying the repaired liner once more. During this time, Roan, who'd been gifted a toy chainsaw by a friend, could be found wandering around the meadow where Luke worked, chopping everything that got in his way.

Along with pond digging we began work on a fixed nature route around Wild Finca, our vision that one day we could offer tours of the land. We created a giant bee hotel; the frame made from scrap wood, filled with wood that had been drilled full of holes, plus canes and stems collected from around the farm. It looked tremendous until Chula used it for a scratching post, felled the whole thing, and we were forced to restyle it as a log pile. Despite her tendency for destruction, we'd begun riding Chula and she was as docile as we could have hoped her to be. Roan was smitten and especially enjoyed the fact that from the seat on her back he could reach the cherries on the trees along the bottom pathway of the Loop.

And all the time we spent on the land allowed for us to learn more about it, and to see when and where the animals should be moved. But knowing and doing were two different things, for while the horses were now fully on board with our regular field changes (the Asturcóns trusted to follow wherever Chula was led), the sheep were another story entirely. Bucket training was a constant dance of one step forward twenty steps back, for Rameses and three black sheep (both literally and metaphorically) would inevitably wreak havoc at some stage of the move, resulting in sheep all over the place. The only reliable follower was Old Mamma, but she didn't hold enough influence to ensure the flock would stay the course on the longer moves. The rest would follow to the point of exiting the field but then something would spook them, or they'd get cold feet, and they'd disappear in the completely opposite direction to the way we wanted them to go. Oftentimes it would take multiple attempts to get them all in the correct field, and on some occasions the flock would end up split between fields overnight.

During one move, Luke was at the front with the bucket, Old Mamma at his heels, and I was left to bring up the rear when Rameses became suspicious turned about and ran straight at me. In his bid to get back to the field from where he'd just come, my leg got caught between his head and horn. Undeterred by the weight he'd picked up, Rameses continued making his break and somehow, I managed to roll myself out. I was lucky to walk away with just a fist sized black bruise on my inner thigh. We spent many more moves trying to race around the farm in an effort to cut them off or chasing after them as they headed for the village, without exception, always in the complete opposite direction to our intended field rotations. The neighbours would take these rogue sheep events with good grace. In fact, it turned out to be a nice way of meeting a lot of the village that we hadn't yet been introduced to.

Unfortunately, that good grace meant we too had to be understanding when their animals ended up in our pasture. However, the morning I looked up from the kitchen sink to see Olaya's tenant farmer's bull in our vegetable patch, head lost amongst the lettuces, was a step too far. Without thinking I ran into the veg patch, grabbed a stick as I went through the gate nearest the house, and charged at the creature, shouting and waving my newly acquired stick. He had the good grace to lift his head but didn't move, and so I'd whacked him across the bum with my stick. It hadn't even occurred to me that he might not take kindly to my charge, for I was more concerned for my vegetables. The bull neither put up a fight nor turned tail and ran, but thankfully he did acquiesce my request and exit the way he'd come. He retreated through the gate, now splintered and hanging off its hinges, onto the driveway, taking a left turn to Olaya's.

Runaway livestock may be part and parcel to rural living; however, extensive damages were not. The problem with the wildlife friendly and low-stocking approach we were taking at Wild Finca, was that the grass really was always greener on the other side. We saw Olaya the next day and I'd relayed the story to her. As it turned out, she was even less pleased with her tenant farmer, for after leaving us the bull tried to get back to its field via a short cut through one of her gates (which now looked in a similar state to ours), squeezing down the narrow space between her parked car and the fence line, resulting in a large dent on the bonnet and a severed wing mirror.

As for the sheep we realised that what we needed was more sheep on our side, so that Rameses and the three black ewes had no choice but to follow. So, to increase the peer pressure we started the process of reintroducing Blanca to the flock. By this point she was on two small bottles a day, which was more due to Roan's insistence on being the one to feed her rather than sustenance requirements, for she was now grazing. Early attempts at reintroduction failed outright, with her always returning to the top of our stairs, sat in a pile with the dogs. A look of, 'I've had a lovely day grazing with those sheep, thank you very much, but now I'm home,' across her face. And so, we bought a new sheep to keep with Blanca in the barn, and gently remind her that she was in fact a sheep, with the plan to reintroduce the pair of them once they'd bonded. We named her pal Dingle (because she came with a horrendous amount of dingleberries on her bum), and Dingle took to Blanca immediately by following her, and as a result us and the dogs. We just hoped that Blanca realised she was a sheep before Dingle decided she was a dog/human.

Fortunately, the plan worked, and when Blanca was re-re-(re-?) introduced to the flock, along with her shadow, Dingle, the pair stayed and joined Old Mamma as first to the bucket and the helm of moves. And slowly but surely the rest began to follow the new pack leaders. Whilst moving our animals as often as we did should have stopped them from wanting to escape to greener pastures, it also played an important ecological role for it mimicked what would have happened in the wild. In the wild prey, such as sheep, would be kept on the move by predators, such as wolves. And why was being kept on the move important? So that the floral diversity was maintained, and so that the animals didn't get sick from eating on top of their own poop.

Growing up, I'd kept horses and one of the accepted parts of horse ownership (that I can attest to, having spent many hours of my youth doing so) is poo-picking. Now if you are going to overgraze your animals (a good indication of overgrazing is a field of short grass and low floral diversity), then you are essentially letting your animals eat their dinner off their toilet, however much you poo-pick. But for some reason this is the landscape we have become accustomed to keeping our animals in, and to counteract the problems that come from keeping animals in such an environment we worm them. Ironically worming animals has become synonymous with keeping them healthy, but the standard de-wormers on the market pass through to the dung making the dung toxic to all dung dwelling insects. One of the most crucial of those is the dung beetle, a remarkable little creature critical to the breakdown and recycling of dung back into the soil. Essentially worming is crashing our clean-up crew population, meaning the crap doesn't break down, resulting in even more poo-picking. It's a vicious cycle.

So, we'd asked ourselves, how had it been done before chemical de-wormers were invented? And that was when we stumbled across the concept of medicine fields. Medicine fields are meadows with huge plant diversity, where the animals can self-medicate on natural forage. Birds-foot Trefoil, Plantain and Chicory are just three plants known to reduce worm burden, for they make the gut inhospitable to worms, and for centuries people would maintain these diverse plots and allow their animals to graze in them on a regular basis so that they could maintain a healthy diet.

But to obtain this diversity in the first instance the grazers needed to be moved regularly, and their population numbers controlled. Both things that an apex predator could ensure, and here at Wild Finca that should have been the wolf, but without him it would need to be us.

At last, it felt like we had a pretty good rotation schedule set up, and the animals got used to the movements so were becoming more amenable. There were the odd slip-ups, when a black sheep rebelled or the fencing went down, so adaptability was still key. However, the methods were already starting to pay off for the health of our animals. Our shearer told us that our sheep were the healthiest he'd shorn in the area! (Please excuse the shameless brag but we'd stood a little taller after that comment.)

Chapter 34

Summer Arrives

We picked wild cherries from the old tree on the boundary of our furthest lands. Luke would lift Ro into the higher branches to get the plumpest fruits, but few made it back to the ground and fewer still made it home. On our wanders I'd make small wildflower bouquets from the meadows, full of blues and purples and yellows, a little sprig of summer that I would pop in jam jars around the house. And we made our best batch yet of Elderflower cordial.

We found our first Chicken of the Woods. A prime specimen, on a cherry tree behind the builder's merchant, and I replicated Jack's chicken curry. We deep cleaned the rabbit hutch and found five extras. We'd an inkling they were in there, due to a few weeks of nest building and the whisper of a miniature leg flashing across the back of the hutch. It was a joy for me and Ro to hold them, while Luke decanted the old bedding straight to the vegetable patch. The cyclical nature of keeping them was very satisfying, for there was now no such thing as a weed; everything from the veg patch, plus veg kitchen scraps, were rabbit food, and as soon as it was passed through it could be put straight back onto the raised beds. Of course there was never enough poop, and with courgette, pumpkin and patty pan plants ready to go in, Luke had taken over Elias's job of the previous year: running up and down the hill to Olaya's with a barrow full of 40kg of manure (the uphill part done when the barrow was full). Sadly, we were seeing less of Olaya now that Alberto was living there. My trips with Roan had ceased after being invited into the once clean kitchen to find the floor littered with cigarettes butts, one of which had ended up in Roan's mouth.

On the hottest days we headed down to our local swimming spot on the river, where Roan would practise blowing bubbles in the clear shallow waters, whilst Luke ventured further out to the deeper faster creases looking for Trout and Atlantic Salmon. He would glimpse them, but the waters were still too cold to stay submerged for long periods of time, and the current would often take him downstream whilst the powerful fishes' muscular bodies allowed them to stay in the same spot.

There was a noticeably larger number of fledgling birds about this year compared to last. A pair of Black Kite fledglings appeared from the nest we failed to locate in the forest, the dried-out thistles we left standing (much to our neighbours' chagrin) attracted endless feasting finches, and the Swallows fledged two successful broods from their muddy nest (materials collected from the second pond) that had been built in the old grain silo. We spent afternoons taming the wild brambles along the footpath, which was a riot of butterflies that Ro would chase in that ecstatic manner that only a toddler can pull off.

While we wandered slowly behind him, tucking back escaping tendrils that reached out to grab at us, those that couldn't be tamed we'd cut back. Previously the council had come and trimmed the lot, but our hope was that in doing it by hand eventually the fence wouldn't be visible anymore, just a living hedge.

On one particularly warm evening, while eating our dinner on the mound, a ruckus of bird shouts drew our attention to the opposite hillside. We happened to be filming our al fresco meal for *Notes from Wild Finca*, so we ran to the camera and zoomed in on the action. A pale morph Booted Eagle was on top of a Carrion Crow, while at least ten other crows were mobbing the pair, three of the neighbour's cows watching on curiously. When we watched the footage back, we realised that we'd caught the encounter from start to finish. The eagle had dropped, like a Peregrine Falcon, out of the sky and onto the unsuspecting crow.

The rest of the crow mob had come to the aid of the attacked, and then a buzzard had arrived to join in with the fun. In real time we'd then watched as the eagle was pushed off its prey and up into the sky, where it tussled for a few moments with the buzzard, before the eagle flew off. Miraculously the dazed crow, which the eagle had hit, got away unscathed.

The Red-backed Shrikes were now up to three nesting pairs, distributed across our thick bushy cover, and they could be spotted perching on any number of perches, including the bean climbers in the vegetable patch. However, they tended to hunt over the neighbouring tenant farmer's cattle.

We'd come to learn that they didn't like dense vegetation, as most of their prey was hunted close or on the ground, and their preferred prey tended to be those found around livestock.

One evening we set up my ancient family tepee, just below the mound, for Roan's first camping experience. We fell asleep to the sound of crickets, calling Barn Owls and the churring of Nightjars, and we woke to cowbells, birdsong and a light mist down the valley. Luke arose earlier to make up hot drinks and brought them to us with a plate of biscuits, the perfect morning after an excitable night with little sleep.

All through the summer the sheep grazed on the common land above Wild Finca, and as their silhouettes began to imprint the orange sky Luke would head up each evening with a bucket of nuts to call them back down to Wild Finca for the night.

When the heat got too much, and we couldn't face the journey down the hill to the river Luke and Roan took to dipping in the pond. They would paddle amongst the Water Lilies and dragonflies, keeping an eye out for the Grass Snakes hunting the froglets, as the chickens enquired with cocked heads from around the water's edge.

We were invited by Jesús, the ex-head of the local police, and his wife, Maria, to their cabana for lunch one day. Their cabana sat within a beautiful mixed fruit orchard, just above

Olaya's, with views straight down the valley to the Picos. Maria had cooked the largest paella I have ever seen, that would have easily fed three times the number of people there, and our sidra glasses were rarely empty. Jesús and Maria were excited to learn more about us and our plans for Wild Finca, a refreshing change from the quizzical confused looks we'd been used to getting when we explained our vision.

Towards the end of July came the magical flying ant day, when males and new queens left to mate and then went on to start new colonies. When the conditions were just right many ant species coincide with this phenomenon, resulting in a blizzard of black gorged on by Swifts, Swallows and House Martins, to Black Kites and Hobbies. More fledglings appeared, like the mystery Pied Wagtail family. Perhaps they nested at Olaya's, but she feeds all the stray cats in the whole valley, so they'd have been lucky to have survived there. We had a wagtail nest the month previous, on the roof of the old farmhouse, but a cat wiped them out in the middle of the night, and we awoke to find the chicks' featherless bodies scattered across the driveway.

By the end of the month the heather was in full bloom up in the monte. The Fennel was taller than our heads, the grasses knee high, and the wildflowers continuing to bloom in their myriad of colours. The Swifts headed off, so did the Egyptian Vulture. Luke managed to finally capture our resident pair of Nightjars on camera one evening, and shortly after they'd fallen silent. The shrikes would soon be gone too.

Into the next month the elderberries ripened, a new food source for the Wild Finca residents, whilst the uncut brambles were now sharing their sweet plump black jewels. On our walks in search of Wasp Spiders, Roan would return without fail with purple cheeks and stained hands from all his scoffing.

The nettle beds started to dry and crackle, the Swallows fed up above the sheep and Lesser Stag Beetles could be found bumbling through the air. In the dry, the new ponds were more than earning their keep, attracting wildlife we'd not documented in the previous years since we first met Wild Finca, like Perez's Frogs from goodness knows where. Dragonflies too, from the recognisable Emperor Dragonfly to the lesser seen Broad-Bodied Chaser. Iberian Grass Snakes could be spotted swimming in the shallows, and Blackbirds, Meadow Pipits and Chaffinches enjoyed bathing at the water's edge.

Our second pond became the go-to place for the Swallow and Martins to bathe, and we would sit by the window in the mornings and marvel at their aerobatics in and out of the shallow water. It also seemed that the days of stressful sheep moving were behind us, as our little flock could be seen loyally following behind Luke and his rattling bucket, the pied piper of the Xaldas. There were certainly less harassed forays into the village in search of errant sheep, but certainly not worthy of resting on our laurels just yet.

The vegetable garden revealed a delightful new inhabitant, a Hedgehog in amongst the bumper raspberry crops. We harvested beetroots, Cavolo Nero, beans, courgettes, shallots, and salad onions by the bucketful. And the pumpkins were beginning to ripen, which we left on the storks to dry until the first frost. Some were already too big for us to have much use for, and they became dinner for the chickens and ducks who gobbled down their innards with relish.

Both last year and now we endured long droughts, not helped by an enduring dry easterly wind. The ponds started to evaporate at an alarming rate; the grass became hay without being cut. Patches of ground began to crack and even our damsons dried in situ on the trees. In mid-September temperatures in the 30s weren't uncommon, our only respite was retreating to our secret river spot and submerging ourselves with the Salmon.

Chapter 35

Build It and They Shall Come

There was barely a single potato. With the success of previous years, we'd gone hard on planting potatoes and dedicated a large portion of the vegetable patch to them with the intention of being completely self-sufficient for the coming year. But apparently the Fossorial Water Voles had caught wind of our plans and decimated the whole harvest. And it wasn't just the root vegetables they'd targeted; they'd taken down several of our fruit trees as well. You could tell the ones that'd been eaten by the voles, for they devoured the roots, and they'd begin to lean precariously, if not fall over completely. One of the reasons we think voles proliferate locally (neighbours complain about them too), was due to a predator imbalance. European Wild Cat was most likely locally extinct, certainly incredibly rare and while some of the feral cats could be classed as hybrid, we'd witnessed them mostly hunting birds. So, the duty of in-house vole control fell to the foxes and owls. We heard the owls most nights, and so we put up Barn Owl boxes across Wild Finca to further encourage them onto the land. We certainly had foxes, we'd lost some runner ducks over the summer to them, although we very rarely saw them. Yet the vole population continued to boom, even more so this year it seemed, and with it our plants were suffering. Not all mind you, the voles had no interest in garlic and onions so both hung drying in the eaves of our hórreo balcony. They also weren't too fussed by the pumpkins, so we had a good harvest of them.

At this time of the year more welcome veg garden guests included Grass Snakes basking beneath the black mats we used to suppress the weeds on unused beds, Praying Mantis, Stick Insects and Glow Worms galore. And after the fuente had dried up over the summer, we'd relocated as many of its inhabitants (mainly Marbled Newts and Dragonfly Nymphs) to two bathtubs we'd placed at the edge of the veggie patch.

Then returned the Fire Salamanders. For most of the year it was very difficult to see them, we'd sometimes come across them under a rock by the stream in the woods but on the whole, they mostly eluded us. However, come the warm wet days of the latter part of the year, there's a feeling in the air and you can just tell that it's going to be a salamander night. Even Roan can now detect the signs. He recently got so overexcited at relocating a Fire Salamander from the road to the grassy verge, that he'd given it a kiss. Not the best idea since Fire Salamanders can secrete a toxic liquid from glands behind their eyes, but fortunately for Roan they hadn't this time. Jesús had not been so lucky, he'd told us one visit to their cabana, back when he was a young lad, after fishing a Fire Salamander out of the fuente to take a look, he'd come out in a horrible rash that got so bad he'd needed to go to the doctor.

A little after the Fire Salamanders, we welcomed back the European Woodcock from the frozen steppes of northern Europe. In Britain the first full moon in November is known as the Woodcock Moon, for folklore tells that it this moon that brings the first fall of returning Woodcock to their overwintering grounds. During this year's Woodcock Moon, while on a late-night airport run, an hour and a bit drive between Santander and home, Luke encountered the definition with nine birds passing over the road ahead of him. Large bodied, bill pointing down, they are quite easy to identify in flight, especially when silhouetted by a full moon. But each year at Wild Finca they are one of the species we are seeing less and less of. Yet the Woodcock hunters remain. For them the Woodcock is a prized hunting species because of the difficulty in shooting them, given their quick zig-zag flight. And I assume they also make good eating.

A hunter, who tended a vegetable patch behind the back of our old rental, and who we'd swapped eggs for bags of kiwis and Romanesco heads, at one of our barter exchanges, had lamented to Luke how few the Woodcock numbers were these days. Along with the Salmon numbers, which were also so low that he'd given up fishing. Surprisingly he was one of the few that blamed the Nestle factory up the road for polluting the water. Of course, none of the fisherman ever questioned the cattle feed lots that spewed manure into the river, or the constant spraying of herbicides and pesticides directly by the rivers. Instead, blame was placed on the 'plaga' (plague) of Cormorants and Otters. The hunter had said how sad he was to have stopped fishing and that one day soon he'd have to give up his beloved Woodcock hunting too.

Another exciting November arrival was the large jelly clumps of frogspawn that started to appear in our ever-expanding fleet of ponds. The exemplification of build it and they shall come. And then, after Luke was finally happy with the re-re-(re?) modelled second pond, we'd watched delightedly as a juvenile Grey Heron caught voles in the field and washed them down with a good drink from the pond. The heron hung around for a couple of months in total, but during that time the pond water levels began to drop again. It turned out that his sharp beak was no match for the liner. And so, again, the pond repairs were added to the mammoth to-do list. Perhaps it is the ponds' proximity to the house, and the fact Luke looks at them first thing in the morning and last thing at night, that despite my best efforts they always managed to jump to the top of said list.

When Luke was working on the far sides of Wild Finca he was relatively unreachable, with no phone signal and being largely out of earshot. Who knows what he may be up to. But by the large ponds we were able to catch him in the act, adding another bank, or dead log. Lifting the liner, crawling underneath to scrape out more soil to alter the gradient, again. The question

I found myself repeatedly shouting from the window, 'Is there not something more important to be doing?'

In fairness the ponds are important to our goals at Wild Finca, and the visiting wildlife to them is testament to that. However, when a storm is due and we have a leaky roof, or the animals have broken out due to a hole in the fence, I feel those are jobs that should take priority.

But this time all jobs were put on hold as Luke's constant toil on the land had taken a drastic impact on his health in recent months. Extreme exhaustion on an almost bi-weekly cycle resulted in him being bed-bound for forty-eight hours. Not helpful, not only for the management of Wild Finca but for our family life too. He scaled down projects, even taking weekends off, and began limiting his daily hours.

Luke hoped to rope in Chula to help with some of the heavy lifting around the place. He'd a vision of doing this work with a large horse and a trailer (our very own Spartacus, just like El Mexicano!), so when the nephew with the horses mentioned an old wooden trailer he just so happened to have for sale, Luke snapped it up. It'd been parked in the village and Luke pulled it back on flat tyres, Roan riding in the flatbed like royalty. But the trailer turned out to be a bigger job than first appeared. We'd stripped the rotten wood relatively quickly, and cut the new wood, but both wheels needed replacing and we just couldn't find any that fitted. So, the metal frame of the trailer sat propped against the side of the old farmhouse until the correct replacement parts could be found. On top of that, the damp started to get to Chula, and she became lame, so the poor old girl wouldn't have been much use, even with a functioning trailer.

Chapter 36

The Big Bad Wolf

Emily and Anne, two Workaways from Colorado, America, joined us for the better part of the month. They were hard workers and wonderful company, and over their time with us they created the most stunning mural on our garage doors.

It was of a little blonde boy, Roan, reaching up to a Barn Owl who was dropping him gifts: a guitar, strawberries, ice cream, pumpkins, flowers, snails; a shower of his favourite things; our sheep, the mountains in the background; the forest and the stream at the bottom; mushrooms and wildflowers; a buzzard surveying the scene from atop a tree stump covered in Chicken of the Woods; and our horses, a peeping badger and a welcome fox.

Seeing foxes at Wild Finca was a rarity but recently we'd started having more regular sightings of the most stunning male. Thick fur, almost golden in colour, we'd seen him on four or five occasions hunting voles in our very top field. A butterfly, a bumblebee and a Barn Swallow joined him. And White Asphodels flowered all over the foreground – a nod to the name we'd chosen for our second son, due three months later.

At the top of the mural the girls had written a motto that they'd been raised hearing: 'Tend to the part of the garden you can reach.' As well as the mural, under their diligence, the vegetable patch flourished, and in their free time, when they weren't climbing or mountain biking, they would join us on our ventures into the woods.

With each trip to the woods, I was becoming more and more familiar with the local edible and poisonous mushrooms. My repertoire slowly expanding with each season, there were now about ten edible species I would happily eat myself. I was always the guinea pig for the first try, Luke next and Roan only in small quantities after Luke and I had eaten them a fair few times without repercussions. It had felt terrifying allowing Roan that first time with the Parasols, and yet aside from a country name we had no idea where most of our groceries came from, or under what conditions they had been grown. A thought which instilled confidence in the action of foraging and feeding, for I knew exactly where it had all come from. However, I still avoided white mushrooms overall, the only exception to this was the Hedgehog mushrooms, whose white spines made them impossible to mix up with anything else. So far this autumn there hadn't been a huge amount about. After one glut of Chanterelles early on, it was too dry and our fungi foraging expeditions had left little to report. A handful of Horn of Plenty here and there, but no Hedgehog Fungus and the boletes we found had all gone over.

Roan loved coming into the woods with me, and he was an excellent mushroom spotter. Perhaps because he was closer to the ground, although he did also have far superior eyesight. He'd treat the whole walk like a treasure hunt. And then, one day, he didn't want to go with me into the woods and it took some coaxing to get the reason from him. At two and a half years old, and having started nursery in Spanish only recently, his language development was understandably a little behind the standard. But as parents of small children will attest, in that interim period of non-perfect verbal communication you learn to understand each other in different ways. And so, we had deduced that the reason Roan didn't want to go to the woods was because of the wolves. If he went to the woods, the wolves would get him.

It wasn't the first time he'd mentioned wolves in this fearful way; there'd been a few new nervous glances out of the window 'in case the wolves were coming', and he'd started asking us to check under the bed too. We assumed it must have been a book at nursery. *Little Red Riding Hood*, the *Three Little Pigs*, and no doubt Spain had a whole library of equivalent titles that told tales of the Big Bad Wolf. We'd asked his nursery teacher, and she guessed that it might be a game they played, where someone played the wolf, and they then chased the others. Seemingly innocuous, but it'd planted the seed of fear for Roan. Along with Emily and Anne we'd managed to coax Ro into the woods that afternoon. After all, there was safety in numbers.

Around the same time, a Swedish PhD student from the University of Leeds, who'd been studying the relationship between the wolf and people in Spain, was visiting nearby. We extended a dinner invitation to her and were delighted when she accepted. Despite having lived in the area for three years and actively investigating the situation, it was Hanna Pettersson who really shone a spotlight on the nuances of it all.

Hanna was a sociologist, whose studies focussed on identifying the best methods to promote positive relationships between people and wildlife in shared landscapes. The fact that some places coexisted well with wolves and others didn't was what had drawn her to northern Spain. Here she was looking to understand what social and ecological conditions were required for coexistence, and she hoped she might be able to deduce from her findings the secret to living harmoniously with large carnivores and how wider society could support the necessary conditions.

Hanna had spent the previous year living in three different rural communities in northern Spain, each representing where the wolf had always been, where the wolf was returning to and where the wolf was predicted to return in the near future. In each location Hanna would begin her investigation by visiting the village bars to speak with the locals over coffee or a glass of wine. Being a blue-eyed Swede, on first impressions she might not have appeared to be the one to gain the locals' trust, but as the daughter of a dairy farmer, who spoke perfect Spanish, and undoubtably her likeable nature, she'd been granted a unique insight into the human-wolf conflict of Spain.

One of her findings was that where wolves had always been the locals were accustomed to the challenges of coexisting with them, and they had adapted accordingly. They kept packs of up to twenty livestock guardian dogs with their flocks during the day and would then bring in their livestock at night. As a result, the number of wolf attacks was low in the area. The wolf may not have been liked, but their enduring existence meant the farmers had refined their techniques of protecting against them over the years, and the presence of wolves therefore felt like a part of normal farming.

However, there was a catch, for during the time Hanna had been in the Sanabria-La Carballeda, trophy hunting was still legal, and she felt that this helped a lot with the acceptance of the wolf. Not only did the income from the hunts support the local council, but the locals also felt that the hunting helped control the population. But now that hunting the wolf was illegal, Hanna was finding the same thing we'd come across (most notably with the mayor by the denning wolves): that wildlife watching didn't benefit local farmers, and the extra work the wolf generated for them was not being reflected in the prices of their products.

Her conclusion for what the human-wolf conflict came down to was quality of life. Those who lived in wolf territory believed their quality of life was significantly less than those who didn't. And with the farming sector dying in the Sierra de la Culebra (the wolf territory she had stayed in), the threat to coexistence with wildlife was even greater, for Hanna believed it represented one of the best examples of a functional relationship between wolves and traditional farming. As a result, for those already feeling the wolf's return, and those anticipating it, they had no interest in entertaining this apex predator's revival. And so, the wolf had come to symbolise the demise of traditional farming.

That evening Hanna had posed to us an interesting question: how could we ensure the future of both wolves and rural communities? How could we use wolves as a vehicle for positive change? Firstly, she said, successful coexistence was only possible through funding. She'd found that funding was primarily available where there was conflict between the wolf and the locals, which meant that the best chance people had of getting the financial aid they required (whether that be to keep guardian dogs or build a barn to keep their livestock in at night) was to live in a community where people were hostile to wolves. The more hostile they were, the more they were listened to.

Hanna also championed the idea of certifying those farmers whose products were sustainable and wolf friendly, so that they might demand a higher price. However, one of the stumbling blocks for this was the marketing of these products. For rural farmers who spent their days caring for their animals, didn't have the time or the know-how to advertise their produce. For this they needed an entrepreneurial middleman and, our friend, who Luke had done the shoots for, had been just the man. Sadly, due to personal reasons, his project never progressed beyond building the website.

Perhaps most interestingly, the solution Hanna deduced from her research was that the problem and resulting solutions shouldn't be focussed solely on the wolf, instead a broader approach to solving more general issues was required. General livelihoods needed to be improved, of which just one part of that was supporting those people to live alongside large carnivores. Hanna's research proposed that whilst a blueprint for what to do wasn't possible, a blueprint of how to work with communities to figure out the relevant solutions to their situations could be created. Solutions that were accepted, legitimate and locally relevant, and of course those solutions would look very different from place to place. Essentially stakeholders needed to feel like they were being heard. From Hanna's experience the most difficult part wasn't working with the communities, the most difficult part was getting the authorities to the table to listen and support.

Storm Barra rolled in with heavy winds, and an estimated 50 litres per square metre of rain fell. Town was chaos, underground car parks flooded, and the main square was underwater. Having been built on a floodplain our local town was now paying for it. We woke one morning without electricity, and checked on the fuse box, located in the washing room outbuilding, to find water gushing through the roof above where the box was kept, box still fizzing and sparking. Amazingly, considering how long it normally took for an electrician to come out to us, and considering the carnage that we knew was taking place in town, someone arrived later the same day and restored power. Meanwhile, the local hospital had to be evacuated, and not for the first time during our lives here, as it had also been necessary in February 2019. According to the neighbours, ten years ago they had left it so late that they eventually had to evacuate on the River Sella in canoes.

Fortunately, Storm Barra was the culmination of a solid month of rain, a month where Luke intended to take a step back from the land so the timing in that respect couldn't have been better, for the weather forced him to. As for Wild Finca, she was now looking the way Luke had before the rains, completely saturated and churned up. Due to some areas not having cover, we'd not been able to move the animals around as often as was normal these days. So, each day we'd taken the horses' hay, they'd have a brief nibble but then it was used as a giant towel as each would lay down and roll in it. Ultimately what the land taught us was that for weather like this, we had too many animals, and as Wild Finca's aim was to benefit nature we made the tough decision to sell some of our sheep (we were now up to sixteen), and Pliny the Asturcón. As a stallion Pliny was a handful, and he'd recently galloped up to Luke and sparred with him in a manoeuvre of dominance, out of nowhere kicking Luke in the chest with his two front hooves. He was too young to be castrated, and we didn't have the time or experience to work with him the way he deserved. So having made the decision to downsize our grazing animals, he had been the one to go.

Chapter 37

The Golden Fox

Typically, the sheep continued to birth, and our flock grew, despite our intentions to downsize. After a surprise arrival at the end of November, six weeks earlier than we'd expected, they'd just kept coming. Because Rameses ran with the flock throughout the year it was hard to know exact due dates and we were still learning the signs of imminent birth. After the rains, to save the land we'd been letting them out onto the common land to graze. Each evening Luke would bring them back down to the field below. However, one night a two-week-old lamb was taken. It had seemed particularly strange for the little lamb was strong and had come down from the monte the evening before in full health, springing from rock to rock, winding in and out of the rest of the flock as they'd all followed Luke down for the night. But the next morning, when Luke went to open the gate to let them up to the monte to browse for the day, the lamb was gone, and the mother ewe was in some distress. There was no sign at all. At the time we believed it to be too strong for a fox, and had instead considered a badger, or even an Eagle Owl, to have been the culprit.

We went on to have a further three more lambs taken from that same field. Two were taken before the ewe had even passed the placenta, the thief more in tune with our sheep lambing than us. For this reason, we could never be sure if they were live-born or not. But with the final lamb, again only a few hours old, we'd caught our golden fox in the act, dragging the lamb across the field in broad daylight. We ran but were too late. We'd heard stories that foxes took lambs, even fair-sized ones, but until this happened, we hadn't really believed it. Having Rameses with the flock full time, lambing was always going to be a guessing game, so from then on, the sheep came in at night. Who needed wolves when you had foxes as big as them!

Although cold, the weather was now clear, and perfect for getting back to the to-do list that had grown exponentially during the rain. Veggie patch prep took priority, something we could all get involved with. Lots of Glow Worm larvae uncovered and gently replaced as we cleared beds ready for planting in the coming new year. Then, on Christmas morning, looking forward to a day off we'd woken up to find Mala Gana's cattle in our top field. Around twenty cows had broken through from the common land, smashing down the drystone wall that divided the two, and were churning up the still waterlogged ground. We chased the cows out and began fixing the walls, whilst trying everyone in the village for a number for Mala Gana. But the replies all came back the same; Mala Gana didn't have a phone, and they would pass on the message. His phone-less existence I both envied and it irritated me, for the cows, having now had a taste for the greener grass of Wild Finca would break in almost daily, and only after a week with the grazing all but gone did Mala Gana collect his cows and move them elsewhere.

With the clear weather, the hunters also returned. The dogs were the first to sound the alarm of the impending driven hunt, and they'd continue with their howling, in synchrony of that of the hunting dogs, until the hunting day was done. At moments like these we were torn between escaping to the sea or mountains (anywhere we could guarantee there wouldn't be hunters), but if we left, we risked leaving our land and animals vulnerable to the hunt. On this occasion we didn't run away, instead we decided to wait it out. We spotted the first hunter easily; orange high-visibility jackets a sore thumb on the scrubby mountainside. He was positioned just above the green route, gun facing directly onto the footpath. Then we spotted his dog, more than two hundred metres to the left of him, running in the opposite direction across our top meadows.

One of the few rules we were sure about was that a dog needed to be within fifty metres of their owner, and they also had to be under control. What struck us as strange was that the dog was a beagle, not the usual spaniel types used for both the boar and Woodcock hunts we'd become accustomed to.

The sound of more beagles yowling through the valley began, and something about the set-up felt different to our previous encounters. We watched as the hunter relocated onto the footpath, gun now pointing into Wild Finca and the field where Chula and Pear were grazing. It was at this point that Luke approached him and politely set out his spiel he'd got so used to relaying. Enquiring what the plan for the hunt was, explaining that this land was private and that there were livestock, children, three dogs and that we'd be walking here throughout the day. How we didn't want anything shot on our land. At this the hunter scoffed 'of course he wouldn't shoot any of us or our animals'. He was there to shoot foxes. And if we didn't want them being shot on our land then we needed to pay to have the land taken out of the 'coto' (hunting reserve), that the land needed to be fully fenced with two-metre-high fencing, and signposted to say it was not for hunting. This was a lot of information we'd never heard before, but with around eighty per cent of Spain a 'coto de caza', which means huntable, perhaps this was the case. (Quite an astonishing amount of land allocated considering only one and a half per cent of the population hunt.)

The Asturian Hunting website states, 'In accordance with current legal regulations, any part of Asturian territory, regardless of public or private property, can be classified as a common hunting area or a special hunting regime area.'

But this surely couldn't be right. And so, we contacted a lawyer who followed Luke on Twitter, to try and clarify the law once and for all. He replied that from his understanding, in principle our land was regarded as common hunting land;

however, if we fenced it and put up signs that entry and hunting were prohibited, we could have it excluded from hunting. No specific height was required for the fencing, unlike what the hunter told us.

Where the hunter was posted was above an old drystone wall which we'd only the summer before re-built. Drystone walls have long shaped the different landscapes of many Spanish provinces, but more recently have fallen into disrepair. It was one of our ambitions to repair and maintain the few that we had at Wild Finca, and it seemed a sad situation if we would have to put in a more secure type of fencing over the top of this just to prevent the hunting.

However, whatever fencing we opted for we would still have to respect the right of way. The lawyer also noted that if we were to exclude Wild Finca from the hunting grounds then we would also be excluded from possible compensation if the animals to be hunted caused any damage.

One of the local hunting arguments is that they provide a service to landowners in terms of 'problem' species control. And they really do regard themselves as 'essential workers'. A video recently shared on Facebook, of a terrified Wild Boar family running down our local high street in the middle of the day, received endless comments of: they're a 'plaga' (a plague), there are too many of them, we need to do something about it. There was no consideration that the boar might be there due to the pressure from hunters pushing them out of their actual habitat. As primarily nocturnal creatures, boar wouldn't have chosen to be there at that time of the day, and research has shown that driven hunts increase the risk of spreading boar over a wider area. (More so even than wolves!)

The compensation was not something that concerned us, for the boars rooting didn't affect our way of managing the land. On the contrary, their work was welcome. Our vegetable patch and food forest were fenced, and they were the only two spots we'd be disappointed to find dug up, but so far, the fencing had deterred the boar. Every now and again they had turned a meadow over, but boar rooting aerates the soil and allows for new species to germinate in the new soil. Our farming neighbours did not feel the same way, however, and claimed that boar diggings affected the traditional grazing requirements of the cattle, and that they destroyed crops. If you have maize or grain crops it can be an issue, but it could also be easily fixed with electric fencing.

For us the boar diggings were creating new habitats. In our circles boar were considered 'ecosystem engineers', and at the Knepp Estate they'd introduced Tamworth pigs as proxy species. Knepp boasts the UK's largest breeding population of Purple Emperor butterflies and the only increasing Turtle Dove population in the UK. Both of these endangered species feed on pioneer plants, which germinate in the exposed earth created by the Tamworth pigs' rooting. The bare soil the Tamworths create is also colonised by solitary bees and ants. In southeast England boar rooting may have decreased the abundance of Bluebells (a scene us Brits have come to view as the epitome of British natural beauty, but in reality, such landscapes are unnatural), but their rooting triggered greater rates of germination of other species. So, the boar visits were fine by us.

As for the foxes, aside from the animal losses they were overall proving to be of great value. Since moving to Wild Finca, we'd lost around fifteen ducks/chickens to foxes, as well as the recent four lambs. Let's say each bird is €7 (the compensation available if we were to go to the town hall about it) and at the moment we can barely get €40 for an adult sheep, so let's say a lamb is around €25. As a very rough guesstimate the total fox damage over the past four years had come to €205. But with Luke's thermal we'd watched the golden fox pouncing on the Fossorial Water Voles, and since moving to Wild Finca we'd lost around twenty fruit trees, as well as all manner of vegetables:

from potatoes and beetroot to cabbages and swedes to the voles' nibbling. We estimated this damage at around €450, not to mention the time spent nurturing and planting the various plants. Unfortunately, the hunters weren't interested in driven vole hunts.

The thought of the hunters shooting our golden fox was rather gutting. It is only right at this point to mention that I have not always been so respectful of these misunderstood creatures for I grew up fox hunting. A sport I took part in for the joy of galloping across the fields on horseback with friends, something I now appreciate didn't require the killing of a fox to do. The age-old explanation: 'have you ever seen a chicken coop after a fox has got in?' my mantra for why we did what we did. I now see fox hunting as barbaric and outdated, justified as a part of British heritage, a part of Britain's cultural identity. But culture shouldn't be treated as a constant. It should be fluid. It should be open to course correcting. Aspiring for good, judging itself when it is bad. Continuing something that clearly no longer has a place in society today, just for the sake of culture, is not acceptable. I like to think I apply this same method to everything in life. We are allowed to make mistakes, learn from them and try to better.

One of my biggest bugbears is people preaching tradition for tradition's sake. I thought this quote in the online magazine *El Mundo*, was spot on:

The privileges of the hunting reserves are based on a law prior to democracy. The Hunting Law dates from 1970 and does not recognise the current needs of a population that practices more and more activities in nature, nor the increasingly generalised sensitivity of those who do not approve of hunting either as a sport or as an effective method for the control of wild animal populations.

The conflict between uses of the great outdoors were becoming even more pronounced, for the previous year six hundred and five people in Spain were shot during hunts. Seventeen were minors and fifty-two died from their injuries. One of the numbers had been a cyclist in a neighbouring province shot dead whilst out for a bike ride.

Unfortunately for us, even though the numbers of hunters applying for permits were reported to be decreasing each year, the hunting on our boundaries would be the last to end for it was so convenient. The guns drive to their set-up points, little to no walking is required, and the valley wood below us is easily navigated. We may look remote, but we are five minutes from a relatively busy little working town. These hunters are not the intrepid hunters of old. These are hunters of convenience and ease.

We breathed a sigh of relief a week later when we woke one morning to see our beautiful golden fox, hunting once more in our top field.

Chapter 38

Killer Vultures

We saw in the New Year with over a hundred fires across Asturias. Not the most promising start to the year. Fortunately, cold frosts doused them, and they didn't take root as they could have. A morning a little while after, Luke was out doing the animals when he spotted some ravens, followed shortly after by a Red Kite, swoop down just the other side of the mountain above Wild Finca. A sure sign of something dead. A couple of hours later the Griffon Vultures got wind of this and began to appear, heading in the same direction as the ravens and the Red Kite. Luke set off up into the monte following them, and he found a small meadow with three cows in it. A pregnant cow, a brand-new calf, and what Luke presumed to be the calf's mother, dead.

The cows belonged to the nephew with the cows, who at the same time had three more cows grazing the little square of land in the centre of Wild Finca. They'd now been there two months, the plot a mud-bath, feeding on hay that'd been cut two summers previously and a handful of beet nuts the nephew would take down when he went to check on them after work each day. Our best guess was that he was using the field like a barn, for there had been no grazing in it for months, and it seemed the same practice was being applied in the field where Luke now stood, watching the vultures do what vultures do best, acting as the clean-up crew.

Unfortunately, Luke and I both predicted what came next. The other brother, the one that kept horses and donkeys, took to Facebook to share the tale of the dead cow. The story translated along the lines; today, two kilometres from town, more than fifteen vultures killed the cow while in labour, and she died. The comments that followed, of vitriol towards the murdering vultures, were difficult to read. They genuinely believed that the vultures were responsible for the death of the cow. Some claimed there were too many vultures, that they needed controlling. Most were calls to 'ecologistas' (a blanket term that applied to anyone from animal rights activists to environmentalists to scientists and a term that Luke and I had been pigeonholed as) asking how they could defend such vermin that were destroying the livelihoods of the famers. (Considering there are now nearly four hundred thousand cows in Asturias, perhaps it is no surprise that there are more vultures about.) One claimed the vultures would be coming for humans next! But the scariest comment was the one that proposed the dead cow be laced with antifreeze.

A report on Spain from 1992 to 2017 showed that over twenty-one thousand animals had officially been recorded as killed by poison baits, but the real figure was thought to be at least two hundred thousand. Of all the birds of prey in Spain, the Griffon Vulture is the most commonly poisoned. Usually, they are not the intended target for the poisoning, instead wolf and fox are normally the main objective, however, hearing more of the local rhetoric when it came to the vulture, it felt to me like this might be changing.

We spent the following days in a state of unease. Whilst normally the sight of vultures overhead was exciting, now it had us holding our breath, hoping they didn't go down and if they did, that they came back up afterwards. The following day a forest guard parked at the top of our driveway. We didn't know whether he was there for the hunt that was running through the valley, or if he was there from a tip-off of the same thing we'd seen on the Facebook thread. Either way his presence gave us a little reassurance.

A week later a tornado of vultures blackened the Wild Finca skies once more. It felt too long after to be a reaction to the same carcass, and sure enough when the nephew came to check on his three cows in the centre field, he told us that Olaya's tenant farmer had a stillborn calf that morning and that he'd left it for the vultures to deal with.

Despite carcass clean-up being a key role the vultures played, which in turn helped prevent the spread of disease in wild and domestic animals, and the pathogenic risks to humans, here in Spain it was illegal for domestic animals to be left out in this manner without permission.

I'd previously covered the story of the reintroduction of the Bearded Vulture across Europe. Part of the story featured the drug Diclofenac, used for veterinary purposes and routinely used by cattle farmers, which had recently been made available to the EU market, despite the European Medicines Agency confirming the risk it held for vultures. This was because Diclofenac had killed 99% of India's vulture population in less than twenty years. The vultures were exposed to it when feeding on dead animals at the dump, and after ingesting Diclofenac, within a few days, the vultures' kidneys failed. Without the vultures to fulfil their role in the ecosystem there was a cascade of major ecological impacts. Dead cattle were left to rot without vultures to clean them up. Packs of feral dogs increased to fill the ecological gap, and the risk of rabies rose consequently. And populations of crows also increased, which raised the risk of infections being passed from them to poultry and humans. As a result, the veterinary usage of Diclofenac had been banned in India since 2006.

Yet, stakeholders from Spain and other European nations argued that cattle carcasses were disposed of differently in Europe to India. They claimed that vultures would not be able to eat meat tainted with Diclofenac. Unfortunately, a young cinereous vulture in the Boumort National Hunting Reserve in Spain was recently confirmed to have died of Diclofenac poisoning. Conservationists believe this is just the tip of the iceberg, and with Spain home to 95 per cent of all Europe's vultures, if this is true, we are on the precipice of disaster.

The nephew also warned Luke to keep an eye on his sheep, for the vultures would eat them given the opportunity. It was the first time the matter had been broached directly regarding their beliefs about the vultures. We'd been reticent to engage for our Spanish was not good enough, our line of work already had us dismissed as 'ecologistas' and being foreigners made our voice even less valid. But Luke had a go. He told the nephew how he'd watched the vultures the previous lambing season, watch our sheep birth from the ridgeline above and once the sheep and lambs moved on, only then had the vultures swooped down to feed on the afterbirth. The nephew shrugged, a sort of 'you'll see' in the hunch and release of his shoulders.

During the whole first dead cow fiasco, Dutch friends of ours who live a few villages down the valley had messaged to ask if we knew about the cow that had been killed by vultures. We gave our version of the story, which our friends accepted as most likely the case, and they'd been keen to share our version of events with their neighbours. But we asked them not to, for ours was a very small community, certainly all the local farmers knew each other, and word would certainly get back to the nephews that we disputed their story of events. You cannot control word of mouth at the best of the times, and this was a conversation that needed broaching gently and with tact. Something we were learning daily how to manage, always made more complicated by the fact that we aren't from here.

Whilst we were trying to live as a part of nature, around us we were experiencing an overwhelming 'us versus them' attitude. These words from a talk by Rebecca Hosking, summarised what we were coming up against perfectly. 'In western thinking, humans are set apart from nature; nature is something to strive against, to conquer, to tame, to exploit or, more benignly, to use for "recreation".'

I could understand people living in cities to feel estranged from nature, but people who had spent their whole lives in the countryside, I found it baffling that they could be so disconnected from nature. It was unlikely Luke and I would ever be regarded as local, but despite how other people described us, we truly cared about the land. We saw the land as sacred, as part of ourselves.

Chapter 39

Asphodelus Albus

February brought cold nights and sunny warm days, which in turn coaxed out the reptiles. Iberian Wall Lizards could be spotted basking on stones by mid-morning, and snow in the Picos forced the Crag Martins down, who we'd see feeding over Wild Finca on still days. Wild birds kept getting caught in the chicken coop, mostly Greenfinch who went in after the grain. They'd be freed, once Roan had been given a close-up of their plumage. The most impressive hostage was a male Sparrowhawk who'd gone in to try and take advantage of the penned in Greenfinch. Leather gardening gloves were required to release him, but again the chance to get a close-up look at such a majestic bird was taken full advantage of.

My second pregnancy turned out to be a lot tougher than my first. I suffered from bacterial bronchitis for what felt like months. I food poisoned myself twice, and there were endless bugs brought home by Roan from nursery that continually knocked me for six. I was due the middle of February, and as the new year turned, and the countdown began, we received some worrying news. A routine blood test had revealed a large tumour on my dad's kidney, and he was swiftly booked to have the kidney and tumour removed mid-January. The surgery was a success, and the tumour, which turned out to be cancerous, hadn't spread. And by sheer luck baby held on until the day my parents arrived to take over Roan duties. Just hours after they'd completed the eight-hour drive from their home in France, my waters broke in spectacular movie-style fashion. A loud pop as I lay in bed my initial thought was that the baby had exploded, it was such a force of pressure. Fortunately, the gush of liquid when I stood up confirmed it was only my waters and not something more sinister but having not had the stereotypical breaking waters with Roan, it threw me a little. From there the contractions ramped up quickly and an hour later I was in hospital. Albus arrived on a full moon after an intense six hours.

We named him after the White Asphodel (botanical name Asphodelus albus), the first wildflower to start appearing in February and, for us, its arrival had come to signal the start of spring. It has star-shaped white flowers which open in succession from bottom to top of its sturdy leafless stem. Each petal is marked with brown veining down the centre, and their long stamens, tipped with reddish orange, extend beyond the petals giving each flower a 'whiskered' look. It's beauty and timing are the reason we named him Albus. A name with roots, quite literally, in the Asturian earth. When we told Olaya the origin of Albus's name, she warned us that they can become a 'plaga', and matter-of-factly said it was best to just chop their heads off. If our neighbours didn't think we were mad before, they probably thought it now.

I was up and about so much quicker the second time around, and it didn't take long for us to get started introducing Albus to his new home. When the Wild Garlic was expected we'd headed into the woods, encouraged by Roan who had remembered better than Luke and me that it was due.

Strolling down we heard our first Grasshopper Warblers. They tended to be our first returning migrants, their unique reeling from the gorse pockets a definitive sign that spring had begun. Under the moss-covered oak and chestnut trees we went, over the bowing barbed wire fence, and through the Silver Birches. The landscape had changed somewhat since our last visit, the vista clearer due to there being no leaves on the trees, and to the fact that there were now quite a few trees down from the storms we had endured over winter.

It was a warm day, spring was in the air and Dog's Tooth Violets peppered the forest floor, with clusters of golden

Primroses starting to appear. We snacked on them lightly and made a note to return a week later, when we hoped there would be more and we could harvest more generously.

Onwards we continued, making our way down the steep bank towards the path, a route for landowners and hunters, the former we rarely see there, the latter we see much more often than we would like. The large boar and fox hunts are noisy enough that we hear them before we see them, and if they are about, we do avoid the woods. But the lone Woodcock hunters with gun and dog are the ones that worry me most. They are silent, until they shoot, and it is in case of their presence that Luke dons a bright red beanie hat, Roan wears a high-vis jacket, and I have wrapped another orange jacket around Albus in the carrier.

We all stumble once or twice, catching our feet on bramble runners. Poor Roan gets caught out most, struggling to lift his little legs above the scraggy undergrowth. But for the time being it doesn't faze him too much, for he is so caught up in showing Luke and me everything. Every bracket fungus, every flower head; he is a natural guide. He points out the Horsetails which he calls the dinosaur plant.

At the path Luke headed on alone, if there was no Wild Garlic the intention was that he would save us the even steeper descent to the water's edge, the sound of the rushing water sounding stronger than I have heard it before. The rain from last week has carved little tributaries all the way down from our land to join the stream at the bottom of the valley, but neither Roan nor Bumba want to be left behind and so, despite the extra weight I am carrying, we follow on slightly behind. We took it slower and arrived just above the stream as Luke was making his way back. The small wicker basket on his arm a quarter full of the long thin green leaves of Wild Garlic. They were just beginning and so he'd foraged lightly, and we planned to return ten days later or so, for then they should be really showing. We checked the basket for Dog's Mercury, a poisonous coloniser of ancient woodland that grows in the same sort of spots. The leaves are quite different to that of Wild Garlic: large oval shaped and long pointed, but it is not a mistake you want to risk making. This is a more important activity when Roan is involved in the picking, his handfuls less selective than ours.

We took the meandering route home, back up to the trodden path, onwards, upwards and then right. Luke pointed out the hole where a Great Spotted Woodpecker nested the spring before, and we passed the old mill where you can find Fire Salamanders, if you lift the right rocks. Bumba started making funny squawking sounds, I think he must have stepped on something, but Roan mistook his sounds for a bird and began searching the treetops.

As we started to make our way back up through the woods Luke spotted something. The rest of us looked to the branch he was pointing to, but we couldn't see anything. And then, just as we had started off again a Sparrowhawk dropped down and disappeared through the trees.

Roan's legs began to hurt and tiredness, and not getting his way, threatened to end the lovely walk we'd enjoyed thus far. Luckily Luke hoisted Roan onto his shoulders for the rest of the walk.

Come March the Tree Pipits arrived and could be heard calling their high, shrill, buzzy 'tzzz'. Then came the Swallows. In the vegetable patch the cabbages went to seed which the pollinators loved. Then suddenly, after high teens and low twenty temperatures for the most part of March, we took an unexpected plunge into minus degrees with intermittent hailstorms, which came as a terrible shock for our fruit trees that had already come into blossom far earlier due to the milder winter. The unseasonal frosts continued into late April with three hard frosts in a row and we didn't have high hopes for the summer fruit crop.

When it warmed up again, the Perez Singing Frogs started to become very vocal in the ponds; Slow Worms joined the lizards basking in the scrubby areas, and on the south facing slopes crickets began chirping on warmer days, their chorus covered every area of grassland, unabated apart from when the temperature really dropped. Swallows returned from spending the winter in Africa as did many others: Melodious Warbler, Iberian Chiffchaff, Blackcaps, the stream of returning migrants became constant.

Chapter 40

Looking Back

As each season unfurled, we began to trust our interpretation of the land more and allow it to shape the decisions we made and the work we did.

Neither Luke nor I had a traditional education for land management. Luke dropped out of university after his class got told by their lecturer to go to Luke for the module on bird ID, because he knew more than the lecturer. And the fact that he'd failed an ethnobotany assignment because he hadn't used any published references, only experiences from his time spent in a remote village in Fiji. For Luke this was the very problem with science; too much reliance on the written word, too little emphasis on lived experience. I, on the other hand, had studied Sport Science at University. Gone on to become a broker in London (of government bonds and interest rates, as pointless as it sounds!) before quitting, doing a ski season as a chalet host, becoming a dive instructor in Roatan, and then heading to manage a bush camp in Zambia, where I'd met Luke. Together we'd gone on to dedicating ourselves to multi-media conservation storytelling.

We were not scientists or researchers or ecologists, but how nature responded was our guide and we were using our first-hand lived experiences, our full immersion in Wild Finca, to help us decide the actions required to ensure the best for nature.

After a year of following a rotational grazing plan we were disappointed for spring to progress and to find that in certain areas we were missing the wildflower diversity of the year before. That first spring living at Wild Finca we recorded Woodcock Orchid, Man Orchid, Provence Orchid, Purple Orchid and Tongue Orchid, and some in very good numbers.

But now, after a year of sticking to the strict grazing rotation there weren't anywhere near as many orchids. We guessed that we were timing the grazing, particularly of the sheep, to coincide with when they would just be appearing. And, as sheep will make a short meal out of such flowers, the flowers were not getting the chance to bloom. We learnt that intuition of movement and reading the land would be a more productive way for what we hoped to achieve. And so, we started to make notes of where and when the orchids were appearing, so that we could plan our grazing around them.

We learnt that some lands held more rain during the wet months, making them boggy and easily churned up, and would therefore need less grazing and much longer rest periods. Going forward we realised that each parcel needed looking at as an individual, and may even need breaking down into smaller sections, depending on things like the time of year and if certain species needed protecting. Were the ground-nesting birds nesting, or were the orchids due? And this type of grazing had a name too, Holistic Planned Grazing. As the Savory Institute described it, 'Holistic Planned Grazing is generally more dynamic, gives greater weight toward real-time feedback and new information, and is designed to give land managers the tools and context necessary to manage complex systems.' It was a method that would allow us to steer our plan based on our own experiences and learning.

As well as our methods our vision had altered somewhat too. We'd started out wanting to revert to some sort of untouched past, but when you start down that line of thinking how far back do you go? So much had been altered by human intervention it was hard to distinguish what 'untouched' should look like. Something Hanna Pettersson said on her visit had stuck with me, 'We should look back for inspiration, but we shouldn't look back for a blueprint, because things keep changing. What is natural or nature to one person is different to another.'

The opportunity for me to look back for that inspiration came in May. Less than twenty kilometres from Wild Finca there's a Palaeolithic cave art site, named Tito Bustillo, which has paintings that are around thirty-three thousand years old.

The cave was discovered in 1968 by a group of potholers who'd rappelled down a natural chimney that connected the outside with a huge limestone cave system below, carved out by running water more than two hundred million years ago. The group had been wandering amongst the epic galleries of stalactites and stalagmites when, in a large open space within the cave, the beam of a flashlight illuminated an astonishing scene on the wall. Appearing through the darkness were herds of wild horses and Reindeers with curved antlers. It turned out to be one of the best examples of Palaeolithic cave art in Asturias, and one of the most complete sites to exist on the whole of Spain's northern coast.

We were led by our guide along the tunnel created since the discovery of the cave, and through several doors fitted to maintain the natural climate in the cave. The route followed the old river course from the outside, to what is known as the East Gallery. Our guide pointed out the original cave entrance, (which had been a primitive living area, identified as such by the bones and tools found there) but which had long since been blocked by a landslide. It was probably the main reason why the site was not found sooner, with the sole remaining access point available only to the most adventurous.

At a point just beyond the original cave entrance, the guide stopped and turned off his torch. After a minute the guide turned his torch back on, revealing the Main Panel; a panorama of animals depicted in colours of violet, blacks, reds and browns. Immediately my eye was drawn to the black outline of a horse's head and quickly after, on the right of the panorama, to a distinctive purple horse outlined in black. The details in the representations were breathtaking, created from minerals such as charcoal, copper oxide and ochre, as if drawn from photographic memory. The guide motioned for us to move closer and crouch down and using the shadow of his finger he traced further images for us to see, the dichromatic Reindeers and some more horses.

It is believed that man first appeared on earth around three million years ago, and with them began the first episode of human life, named the Palaeolithic. This era is split into the Lower, Middle and Upper periods, and archaeologists have since identified that Tito Bustillo was in use for most of the Upper Palaeolithic. The rock art examples cover a period of around 35,000 to 14,000 years ago, and it is widely accepted as one of the most astonishing friezes of cave art from the era, with large polychromatic animals covering other paintings and engravings of earlier times. Almost a hundred representations have been identified on the panel made up of deer, horses, Reindeer, Ibex, Bison and one Auroch (ancestor of the domestic Ox).

The guide drew our attention to the fact that the horses were one behind the other. That the two big Reindeer were facing each other, and the small Reindeer were in a line. Clearly these were not animals drawn in isolation, this workmanship was depicting a scene. And it is believed that the species illustrated were the ones the artists lived alongside and depended upon. However, not all the animals they hunted and fished are represented, and so it is understood that the selection of animals chosen were not determined solely by their dependence on them for survival.

Some believe that the pictures inside Tito Bustillo are all connected and form a whole, however, too much has been lost through floods, rock falls and the growing of stalactites and stalagmites to prove this theory. So why did they paint and engrave the imagery they did? We can only guess. But one thing it did show was that there have never been humans without grazing animals.

Chapter 41

Other Inspiration

It wasn't just looking backwards that inspired us moving forwards. In mid-April we embarked on a research trip/working holiday, our first stop a family-owned farm just outside of Madrid, called Vaca Celta. Like us they had two boys, a few years older than Roan, and they'd taken on their home with a vision very similar to us at Wild Finca. Their 'conservation grazers' were forty Cachena cows, who they moved daily around their thirty-hectare finca. They spent time with their cows, getting to know them and their land, and based their moves on what they saw. Their commitment was to take care of these animals and these lands in the best way they could, and it was clear that their intentions were creating the most amazing habitat. Woodchat Shrikes chattered from the trees, and the calls of Cuckoos and the song of Nightingales accompanied us throughout our visit.

What differed from Wild Finca was that they sold their meat, which they did to a private mailing list who believed in their methods. In fact, their produce sold within a day of notice being sent out. We shared a steak with them the evening of our visit, cooked over a wood fire, it was utterly delicious. One hundred per cent grass fed, on an uncountable variety of different plant species. We added our name to the mailing list the very next day.

Our next stop was Rewilding Portugal's Greater Côa Valley project, where they were creating a 120,000-hectare corridor for Iberian wildlife. We arrived in the height of spring, and the mix of river gorges, rocky heathlands, oak forests and scattered fields, that made up the area, was a kaleidoscope of colour. It was all being protected and nurtured to create a wildlife corridor that connected the Malcata mountain range in the south with the larger Douro Valley in the north. To help support Rewilding Portugal's nature restoration they'd recently introduced Sorraia horses, a native Portuguese breed reminiscent of the wild ancestor of the Iberian horse. Like our Asturcóns, the Sorraia were perfectly adapted to their surroundings, and we were fortunate enough to see them with the Team Leader of Rewilding Portugal, Pedro Prata. The newly introduced herd were a while off being as wild as their ancestors, and Roan was permitted perhaps a little too close to them as the horses had approached and sniffed us curiously for treats.

It was not the only re-introduction Rewilding Portugal were working on, there was another planned for the near future, with each species selected from historical information regarding what had previously existed on the land. One of the main guides for this selection process was a prehistoric rock-art site, located where the Côa River Valley confluences with the Douro exists one of the world's biggest open-air sites of Paleolithic art.

We loaded the minibus in the village of Castelo Melhor and set off along the dirt track for the rock art of Penascosa. The bumpy route wound its way through a wide valley area amongst almond and olive groves, with large vineyards covering the opposite side to the one we drove, and as we went our guide told us how the art we were about to see ranged from between 30,000 and 12,000 years old.

Prior to the discovery of the Côa Valley open air rock art, it was generally assumed that Palaeolithic rock art was restricted to caves and rock shelters. However, it is now believed that for the most part open air rock art has been destroyed by erosion, and it has only survived in the Côa Valley thanks to specific climatic and geological conditions.

We parked up by the river and as we made our way over to the rock Roan pointed out two large birds overhead. Typically, Luke had left his binoculars on the front seat of the car back at the village (inevitable that something gets forgotten when you are wrangling two little ones) but fortunately the birds came lower, and we were able to identify them as a pair of Black Storks. It was a rare sighting, for these endangered birds are suffering due to being outcompeted for nesting sites. The rewilding team had been involved in artificial nest building to help them out, so we knew they were in the area, but our guide was disappointed to see the pair. One of them should have been on the nest by then, he told us, news that turned a sweet moment sour.

But that feeling of delight quickly returned as we approached the first rock face, there is something very humbling about being in the presence of such ancient art. The rock outcrops are positioned like an amphitheatre around the river, the art carved into the vertical schist slabs.

One of the rock plates featured a mixed herd of incredibly clear horses, Auroch and deer overlapping and all facing in different directions. On another there is an Ibex drawn in both profile and head on, apparently rather unusual for the period it is from. There are also examples of the rock art depicting movement of the animals, achieved by the representation of a single animal body with two or even three heads in successive positions of its movement. At Penascosa we saw an example of this in the engraving of what looks like a three headed horse. Apparently when seen through the flickering light of a campfire, the image gives the illusion that the horse is moving its head up and down.

Large herbivores dominated the representations and like at Tito Bustillo, they tended to be in groups. I found myself asking the same questions as I had done at Tito Bustillo. Why were animals engraved on rock surfaces? Was it for artistic expression? Was it to pray for hunting success? Or was it a message to others passing by, that these animals roamed here? Whatever the meaning, significance from that last question was being drawn.

While the Ibex and Red Deer still existed, and the prehistoric horses now returned to the land in the form of the Sorraia horses, the next intention for Rewilding Portugal was to introduce a proxy species for the Auroch, the ancestor of all cattle. Hunted to extinction in 1627 its DNA still runs through a few ancient original cattle breeds, and by back breeding the closest relatives of the Aurochs they had created the Tauros. For Rewilding Europe, the final goal with the selectively bred Tauros was for wild herds, of at least 150 animals, to exist across Europe.

Luke came away from our trip with his heart set on cattle, but I wasn't quite there yet.

Chapter 42

The Wild Finca Guide

As the months warmed up, we spent more and more time outside. We spotted our first Bee Beetle, feeding on a Scabious. Orchid species number six and seven for Wild Finca appeared in the form of the Sombre Bee Orchid and the Marsh Orchid, which popped up beside the pond below the giant pear. At Roan's third birthday party, a balmy June day, a large Grass Snake caught and ate a Spiny Toad in the purple sprouting broccoli bed. It took about an hour for the snake to fully devour the toad, and the scene provided quite the nature documentary experience for our guests. The Grass Snake continued to hang around for a few months after, and we hoped his diet included the voles that repeatedly devoured our root vegetable crops.

June was also the month we welcomed a group of nine ecologists from JNM, a youth movement from Belgium that focussed on three central themes: nature study, nature management and the environment. We'd met the group leader, Ewout, a few years previously at a photography festival in Antwerp, where Luke had given a talk, and we'd stayed in touch ever since. A photographer/graphic designer, Ewout had also been helping us put together a 'Wild Finca Guide', funded by a grant Luke had secured with the Emergence Foundation. Through our filming of *Notes from Wild Finca*, we'd come to realise that one of our goals was to create Wild Finca as a point of inspiration and guidance. We wanted people to be able to take away ideas from our project and apply them in their own lives, whether that be on their apartment balcony, back garden, the grass verge near their home or even their farm, basically whatever space they had access to. In time we hoped to inspire a network of Wild Fincas to spring up across Europe, stepping stones for nature to move between, places for people to immerse themselves and learn. Something that didn't require you to have a landscape-scale project to get involved with.

As storytellers by trade Luke and I were beginning to see the potential Wild Finca could have as a tool to connect people to nature. Be it virtually (storytelling on social media, or the films we made documenting our life at Wild Finca) and now, through visiting in person. And so, the Emergence Foundation funds were put towards information booklets in both English and Spanish and three information boards to go along the nature route we had already begun developing. Luke's guiding for the big stuff (wolf/bear/wild cat) had stepped up, and amongst it he'd also guided his first few day-tours of Wild Finca which had been well received. It led us to setting ourselves the long-term goal of being able to offer the same to a wider audience, schools and universities a key aim. Ultimately, we wanted to make the knowledge and landscape of Wild Finca accessible to everyone.

It was therefore fitting that Ewout's group were the first to stay with us, camping below the mound for the week. In exchange for this and guiding, they helped Luke build a new pond (of course!). But it wasn't only Luke who took on the role of guide for the group, for Roan actively stepped into the role alongside Luke. On their trip to Sueve it was Roan who spotted the group their first Iberian Rock Lizard. He also led the rock-pooling activity at the beach and was chief snake-spotter on their river walk.

Alongside the conservation work and the expeditions, there were a few experts amongst the JNM group, including a bat expert who worked for the Bat Specialist Group of the IUCN Species Survival Commission. With his bat detector he doubled the Wild Finca mammal count, identifying sixteen different bat species: the Soprano Pipistrelle, Common Pipistrelle, Kuhl's Pipistrelle, Brown Long-eared Bat, Grey Long-eared Bat, Leisler's Bat, Noctule, European Free-tailed Bat, Greater

Horseshoe Bat, Geoffroy's Bat, Greater Mouse-eared Bat, Blyth's Myotis, Daubenton's Bat, Serotine, Barbastelle and Escalera's/ Cryptic Myotis. Despite making up one fifth of all terrestrial mammals, bats are some of the most endangered of the world's creatures so to have so many was a good indicator of the rich habitats at Wild Finca. The Grey Long-eared Bat was specifically associated with wildflower meadows, a good reflection of Wild Finca's meadows the bat expert told us.

June was also the month for fledglings. Robins and tits chattered around the house, and a Common Redstart family took to the homemade box we erected on the back of the hórreo, successfully fledging five young. Two Pyrenean Lilies, a species we'd not seen before, appeared in the area we call Los Pinos, an area that'd previously been largely gorse and rough grass, but where two winters ago Luke had hit with his brush cutter. The following spring there had been a few irises, but this year, along with the correct grazing schedule, it was now a sea of irises, with over seventy flower spikes across the area, plus Eryngiums, Thistles, the two Pyrenean Lilies and much more.

Unfortunately, at the same time, a new dog owner moved into the village over the hill from us and insisted on letting her two greyhounds run completely free across the lands surrounding the green route. These walks took place three times a day (5 a.m., mid-afternoon, and late evening), often with the dogs arriving ten minutes before their owner, worrying the cows and calves on the common land before eventually responding to the owner's shouts. Only to touch base with the owner, before racing off once more. The electric fences had no effect on them, and one day we found the remains of a dead Roe Deer fawn on a patch of land just off the footpath, most certainly killed by the greyhounds.

When the dogs first turned up our sheep were grazing far enough away from the footpath, but as the grazing rotation took them closer, we got more and more nervous. The inevitable eventually happened, typically on the day we were due in the city for meetings about renewing our residency. As was becoming the ritual the 5 a.m. dog walk triggered our dogs and we'd woken when the event must have occurred, but as it was still dark Luke had to wait for the sun to rise before he could go and check on the sheep. As predicted, they weren't in the field they should have been in, the field above the pathway, and he eventually found a handful of them lodged in thick brambles half-way down the valley. Another handful were caught in scrub eight hundred metres in the opposite direction. There was a lone sheep here, and a pair as high up the rocky common land as they could go, but no sign of Blanca. Having been raised with our dogs, and therefore with a complete lack of fear of them, we feared the worst. And then, just as Luke was about to give up, he spotted her at the centre of a bramble bush, unable to move.

Luke contacted the local Guardia to find out what the situation with dogs worrying livestock was, and it was explained that any dogs off the lead had to be within fifty metres of their owner and under control. The fine for not respecting this rule was two thousand euros. When he heard our story, the Guardia had gone round to the greyhound owner's house and given her a warning. We did not see those dogs again for months, and when they returned, they were as good as gold, off the lead but never more than twenty metres from their owner. We were lucky this time.

Chapter 43

A Run of Bad Luck

July started in search of Wasp Spiders and Praying Mantis, and we hand-tamed the wild brambles along the public footpath, in the hope that the council wouldn't need to with their strimmers and chainsaws. Always cutting back too far, a problem at the best of times but especially now for the Great Tits were on their second brood in the holly along the green route. Then we'd returned to the UK for the reminder of the summer. Work, and to introduce extended family to Albus, were the reasons behind the almost two-month long trip. It was too long to be away from home, and we struggled, missing our wild paradise. However, there were family catch-ups galore, and we did spend a particularly special afternoon at Lemsford Springs, a small nature reserve where Luke had spent many years of his youth helping out. It was also a place we'd both filmed a short film on Water Shrews for BBC *Springwatch*, so it was only right we took Roan and Albus. Together we raked cress, and Roan found a Bullhead: a small strangely shaped catfish that to his delight he was allowed to hold. The highlight of the afternoon was the boys getting to watch science in action, with the colour ringing of a Green Sandpiper which Roan released afterwards. Last year one of Lemsford's Green Sandpipers headed south to Santander, not too far from Wild Finca. Maybe on Luke's next birthday we'd see the Roan-ringed bird in our pond.

But even the highlights had happened under a shadow, for we'd left Wild Finca in the care of some very unqualified house-sitters. We'd interviewed them beforehand; they told us they had experience with livestock, and they didn't work so the less than perfect internet and poor phone signal hadn't phased them in the slightest during our meeting. I'd checked their reviews which were good, although in hindsight had only been for short-term house-sits in towns. But even during the hand over, things had been off. In fact, from the minute they arrived there had been an uncomfortable and tense atmosphere. They just didn't get the Wild Finca vision and pulled faces as we showed them round. They saw it as a mess, they'd complained about the brambles, which according to them you could catch tetanus from, therefore letting them grow was both irresponsible and dangerous. The days we crossed over they did some odd things, like race us to the chickens to collect all the eggs before we could. The morning we left, there'd been some plums on the tree that Luke had pointed out to the house-sitters and he'd explained that he was leaving them to the last minute to ripen so that we could take them on our travels for the boys. When Luke went to pick them, they were gone. As soon as we had driven out, we received a message about there being a problem with the water, so en route to the ferry we troubleshooted what it could be. They never let us know the issue was resolved so we spent the whole ferry journey stressed, only to arrive to a message saying 'all fine'. But from then on, the husband sent us daily aggressive messages about the bad phone signal, the insects, just a few of the uncountable complaints they had about things that were completely beyond our control. And even though we'd left them with our run-around car as part of the deal, when the phone signal went down, they demanded what they were expected to do in an emergency.

The day we arrived home, after a thirty-hour ferry and already on high alert after the difficult messages that'd been exchanged daily during our absence, we arrived to a locked house. They knew we'd not taken keys; our spare keys had been moved from where we'd left them, and they were uncontactable. With hungry, tired, hot babies we had headed into town for lunch, and only four hours later had they returned to let us in. What met us was utter devastation. The vegetable patch had been stripped, and nothing watered during our absence. Our winter stored onions and garlics all gone. Most of my dried stored foods gone. They had quite literally eaten us out of house and home. Our instructions to help yourself to things that will go over in the garden, clearly misheard as 'help yourself to whatever you want, from wherever you find it'. And the house was left in a state: covered in mouse poo, stains across the walls and ceilings where the house sitters had swatted insects and just left them. For months afterwards I'd beaten myself up about how we had got them so wrong. They'd been patronising through it all, but we hoped that once we were gone then perhaps it would get easier for them. It felt like they didn't like us and so had actively tried to screw us over. One saving grace was that the animals had been okay, although perhaps not cared for and largely ignored, they'd been fed and watered. The whole experience left us never wanting to leave home again.

After our return we continued our string of bad luck. Luke and Roan moved the sheep a couple of days later and they found the remains of our beautiful golden fox. He'd been shot whilst we'd been away, and we were devastated. We'd come to know this fox, understand him. We'd adapted our way of sheep keeping because of him. He'd taught us so much about co-existing. But his loss was not the only we encountered thanks to that gunshot. The left remains of our beautiful fox triggered a further devastating chain of events, for his rotting carcass attracted blowfly and, unbeknownst to us, the flock had picked it up whilst grazing the same field. Still unaware of the situation, Luke and Roan had moved them to the field above us, where the land meets the common land. And there we'd kept an eye on them from our bedroom window. Having just arrived home, and with a lengthy to-do list, we skipped a day checking on them more closely, and the day after we went to move them only to find half the flock dead and the remaining half on death's doorstep. It took us a while to figure out what had happened, and even to this day we aren't a hundred per cent certain of it all.

Our immediate reaction, and that of Pablo's as well, was that it had been a wolf attack. Due to the positioning of the bodies, all lined up against the fence, as if chased down by a predator. But the park rangers we contacted said it was impossible, as there were no wolf reports in the area. And so, it was decided it was a dog attack, which our camera trap on the edge of the field later confirmed. Footage of a large dog (one we knew to be aggressive from our previous encounters with it on the footpath) entering and leaving during the time frame of the deaths. We tried to get in touch with a vet, but it was a holiday, and we could find no one willing to come out. And so, we moved the sheep and watched them until we started to realise that the flies that followed them were different to usual, and greater in number than normal. What drew our attention to them was the huge numbers of Asian Hornet hanging around the sheep. My initial reaction was that the Asian Hornets were attacking the sheep, but then, when we got closer, we realised the hornets were in fact hunting the blowfly. When we finally realised that the dog attack was only half the story and that we were also experiencing a case of flystrike, we soon realised that we were now in a race against time.

Luke began shearing and treating the remaining nine sheep, and in the process he made the devastating decision to euthanise two. It was touch and go with the last seven but somehow, they pulled through. And, by some miracle it was the tamest of the flock that survived. Blanca and Dingle came out the best of all. We wondered if perhaps they hadn't run from the dog, having grown so used to our own, and so hadn't been attacked. Therefore, they didn't have the open wounds that helped multiply the blowflies so quickly. We were also experiencing unseasonably warm and wet weather for the time of year which had clearly fuelled the flystrike. A series of unfortunate events, triggered by the loss of our fox and compounded by climate change and an out-of-control dog. We will never know the whole truth but that was the takeaway we came to. Either way man had been responsible for this causal sequence. From shooting the fox, to the dog off the lead, to the bigger, more pressing matter of our abnormal weather.

Luke spent weeks after the incident waking up in a cold sweat, thinking flies were laying eggs in his body. He was in such distress after the event I could easily see why it is reported that farmers die of suicide at almost twice the rate of the general population. Imagine if farming was our sole livelihood. I certainly don't think we have the mental capacity to handle it. We may have our issues with some of the methods of the farmers around us, but we certainly don't envy them.

Chapter 44

Little Green Yummies

In September we said goodbye to the Black Kite and, almost on the same day, welcomed back the Red Kite. It was still scorching so we'd regularly head down to the river to cool off, Roan now snorkelling with assistance from Luke. One afternoon, while Albus and I hung out on a picnic blanket on the bank, Roan and Luke went in search of Eels. Suddenly, a scream of panic from Roan and the pair came splashing and spluttering back to shore. A furry head, they reported, had appeared suddenly in the crystal waters. I sent Luke back to fish it out, the best course of action to hopefully prevent nightmares for Roan, and confirm what exactly it was for Luke said there was the possibility it might have been a bear. Caught in the eddy below a large rock, it turned out to be a boar's head. No doubt a victim from the previous day, the first day of the hunting season.

Later in the month we hosted a group of four eighteen-year-old kite surfers from Germany, who restored my faith in humans. They'd just left school and were travelling around Spain in two campervans, which they parked in the driveway. For their Workaway hours they smashed the to-do list, insulating the downstairs barn roof (finally!), building a load of new gates for around the land and they helped us start the process of converting 'the goat palace' from walnut tree back to building. After hours they played paddleball and let Roan join in, which he adored. And in the evenings, we all squeezed around our tiny kitchen table for dinner. With a few evenings spent around a fire on the mound, eating stockbrot, campfire cooked bread on freshly cut hazel sticks, which the boys introduced us to.

Luke later told me that they'd been stoned much of the time, but if that was the case I was none the wiser. I never caught them smoking, neither did they smell of it. They were kind, fun, hard-working and we'd been sad to see them leave. Someone who was not sad was Olaya, who one afternoon stomped round to screech at Luke about the comings and goings of our friends. She didn't like them standing at the top of her driveway (which was also the top of our driveway). In her defence a German couple who we'd had Workaway for a week the month before had chosen it as the site of their daily yoga sessions, a bizarre choice considering the extent of Wild Finca's land, but not exactly illegal. But that was not all, there was more.

She was cross that Luke had retrieved runaway livestock from her land without her consent. The livestock she had no quarrel with; her issue lay with the fact that Luke had entered her land without consulting her. It wasn't worth explaining that as she had spent the last six months intermittently bedridden with back problems, we hadn't wanted to disturb her, for she was clearly on a roll. But the icing on the top of the grievances was the fence, the very first one that we had built, the one that we had walked with her to confirm the line. All memory of this forgotten, only the fact that it did not follow the original boundary remained and she was furious about it.

Maintaining neighbourly relations had always been a priority. Fortunately, in this instance the fence had not stood the test of time well, the cattle had regularly leant against it in their bid to graze our side of the fence, the variety of forage so much more attractive than the poached overgrazed grass on their own side. Plus, the runoff of the water during the rainy months collected in a sort of bog around the fence line, so pretty much all the fence posts were now wobbly. So, it was going to have to be re-done sooner rather than later, otherwise we were at risk of a food forest full of cows.

I'd appeared with the boys shortly after she'd got into her rhythm and at the sight of Roan and Albus we'd been quickly forgiven, which taught us a good lesson. When Olaya got upset about something all we needed to do was use our secret weapons to diffuse the situation. As for the fence, we'd seen to it the next weekend and, with a metal post hitter, and the odd detour into our own plot for sake of ease, we were able to re-lay it to Olaya's satisfaction.

It came time for Chula to move on, her large hooves had become too destructive on the land, and to replace her we bought two Asturcóns from a riding school, called Panchito and Fumo, to join Pear, which meant Roan (led by Luke) and I could now ride out together.

The surviving sheep thrived, although they were now having a few run-ins with Luke after destroying a handful of trees he'd planted and hanging around the edges of his ponds causing damage there. It all felt a bit like déjà vu of the goats.

Our first Autumn Lady's Tresses appeared, orchid number eight for us. The Elderberries began to ripen, and Carlos, who was now full time at the Palacio, invited us around to harvest apples that the owners had no interest in and would otherwise have been left to rot. Thanks to the late frosts we'd encountered at the beginning of the year we'd suffered a summer with barely any walnuts, cherries, peaches, and now our apples were few and far between. But around Asturias there were microclimates and the Palacio, which was only a ten-minute drive and only one valley across, had a different climate and therefore fruit yield to us. With their bounty we made chutneys and apple cakes galore. Closer to home Jesús and Maria invited us to the cabana for sidra and to collect sweet chestnuts from their trees, which were the most plentiful around us. Luke attempted a chestnut flour bread, a time-consuming endeavour, and we agreed that they were better used thrown haphazardly into roasting trays and stews. And then, for the second year running we harvested

Chicken of the Woods from the same cherry tree behind the builder's merchant.

October was a month ripe with home-grown goodies to harvest as well. Our first sweet potatoes and a glut of brussel sprouts, known to Roan as 'little green yummies'. The pumpkins did well like they always did, but this year we'd shaken up the varieties, for the local type didn't taste of much and would grow to beyond usable sizes. Roan and Luke had their fun with those, however, rolling them down the hill or carving faces into them, until they eventually become dinner for the chickens and ducks. For our kitchen we tried the Queensland Blue, an Australian heirloom variety dating back to the 1930s. A striking ribbed blue-green squash with a rich sweet orange flesh that turned an earthy honey flavour when roasted. And the Ute Indian, another ancient variety from the native Ute people who lived in Colorado from AD 1300 to 1881, a grey-blue-green squash with a huge button on the bottom.

With the veg patch overall producing more year on year, we were moving closer and closer to self-sufficiency on the food front. We were learning how to eat seasonally, which had taken some getting used to. Feast or famine. Too much of something so that you got bored eating it, however creative you try to be. Then when you crave something, trying not to give in and buy it from the supermarket, where it has come from some far-flung country, can be extremely difficult. We are so used to having what we want, when we want it. Bananas are one of the foods I haven't been able to give up, too much of a staple for our family especially with young children. But the seasons were beginning to change everything.

These constant climatic changes were hard to keep up with. Not enough water and then too much water. Too hot or too cold. What worked last year for us didn't necessarily mean it would work the next year. Every year, although we inched closer to becoming fully self-sufficient on vegetables and fruit, with these challenges reaching full self-sufficiency across all foodstuffs was a long way off. And there was the fact that we liked diversity. We could turn over the patch to solely five simple crops. We could probably survive on that, but we enjoy cooking. We like different flavours, colours and dishes. There's only so much pumpkin soup or stir-fried greens we can consume in a row. Plus, learning from our potato failures, sticking to just a few simple crops could also be high risk. By planting a variety, we not only offered variety in our diet, but we also spread our bets.

Through all our experimenting Roan and then Albus had been plonked on the ground beside us. Watching as we sowed and harvested. More Luke than me, for I have only truly appreciated the work that goes into the eventual harvest since moving to Asturias and having my own garden to tend. Of Luke's knowledge, I've always been in awe, and he says he learnt in the same way that our boys are doing now. Less active helper, more from just being immersed in it, constantly absorbing the information. And I hope so, for I would love for the process to become a part of our boys' identity. So that when they are older, they have the knowledge to be able to do it for themselves, and hopefully also the passion to want to continue doing it. I truly believe that if we all showed a little more care for where our food came from, and what it took to get to our plates, we would be well on our way to answering a good number of the problems of the world today.

Chapter 45

The Fires

We'd been doing the evening animal rounds. Bumba was acting strangely, he couldn't walk in a straight line and had thrown up. We were trying to work out if the sixteen eggs he'd snaffled from the chicken coop could be the cause. We hadn't collected the eggs yesterday and as we were getting eight a day at the moment, and thanks to the tell-tale eggshells that littered the chicken coop (and the fact Indie and Otis couldn't get in the coop), we'd taken an educated guess that was the number he'd consumed. Can you get neurological malfunctions from eating too many eggs? Or perhaps a snake bite? Indie had once been bitten by a snake and the behaviour wasn't dissimilar. We put him to bed with water and headed to put the ducks and geese away. It was crossing the vegetable patch when we noticed the first wisps rising above the opposite hillside. As we went to turn the dinner off, so that we could walk over and check the damage, the first flames appeared on the crest.

We walked along the green route, checking the Barn Owl box in the centre of Wild Finca with the thermal, and it glowed white confirming that our Barn Owl was in there. Most evenings, once the boys were asleep, we'd taken to watching him hunt out of our living room window. And just the week before we'd watched him one morning, sat on the ledge of one of the other boxes (we now had three in total) while a fox slunk across the fields below, and two Mallards swam in the pond. Along with regular sightings of a pair of foxes, plus boar and a Genet captured on the trap camera at the bottom of Wild Finca, we were feeling quite content that the wildlife was finding us. Word had clearly gone around that we were a sanctuary.

At the bottom of the hill, we took a left to the land we called Adlington Meadows. Roan pointed out the camera trap that earlier in the week had captured a Pine Marten. Luke pulled back the overgrown gorse and brambles, so that we could pass through to the land beyond, which we'd nicknamed the Amphitheatre. A beautiful little meadow nestled between rock, scrub and trees. The previous summer our camera trap here had badger passing through almost daily, so we kept quiet (or as quiet as one can with a Roan and Albus in tow) just in case the badgers were still active on the path. We scrambled up the rocky incline, ducking the low-slung limbs of a holly, before popping out into another small grassy patch. Beyond was scrubby common land, and a sharp descent led to the neighbouring village. The whole time a Blackbird was alarm calling, angry at someone, and we thought perhaps it was us, until Luke spotted an owl in the lone tree. With the sun now set he was just a silhouette, and he flew away from us so quickly that we didn't have a chance to confirm species.

At the ridge of the land, we could now see that the fire had consumed the entire crest of the opposite hillside. It burned brightly with thick white smoke, but we couldn't smell it, indicating that the wind was blowing it away from us. Additionally, it would have to burn through the neighbouring village to reach us. For now, we and our wildlife oasis were safe.

The news from the other side of our neighbouring village was not the same. Our South African friends, who owned a beautiful B&B over the mountain from us, had sent a photo of the same fire we'd just been watching, except it was much closer to them, perhaps a hundred metres or so from their front door. All the fire would have to do was jump a road and they would lose their home.

Every year between 10,000 and 20,000 hectares of land were being burnt across Asturias, mostly in the name of regenerating pasture to create more grazing land for livestock. A study looking into the causes of forest fires in Asturias, between 2002–2012, found that of the 1070 fires that were investigated during that time, 751 of them were set for this reason. It is believed that by burning the gorse and fern the grass will take its place. Yet gorse germinates with fire, and so, in the wake of the fires, more often than not, we were seeing the gorse and other more resilient species, such as Bracken, coming back quickest.

The next biggest motivation for setting the fires was to get rid of brush, both for aesthetic reasons (people thought it looked messy) and in the belief that brush was a fire hazard, and therefore needed managing. But as Alfredo Ojanguren, a professor at the University of Oviedo said, 'one thing that is now dominating the issue of fires and that everyone repeats is that of "the mountain is dirty." Or "you have to remove all that vegetation". There is no more fuel than in a gas station and gas stations do not burn. If they burn it is because someone sets them on fire.'

The other motivations behind the fires, the study found, were to scare away the animals (I can only assume they mean wildlife here) and to make it easier to hunt.

One day, I drove the twenty-five minutes from town to the coast through a cloud of smoke, with the entire mountain range to my left on fire. Ironically it was the same day Roan's school launched a walk to school initiative, to save cars on the roads for the school run and promote good health. That the first morning it took place the town was engulfed in smoke, was a disaster.

A fire on the opposite hillside to us burned for three days, and firefighters spent the night up there monitoring the situation until daylight made it possible for the helicopters to arrive with water. We'd watched as the Red-billed Choughs flew in distressed circles, helpless as their colony burnt, and Luke heard on his birding group that our most local Egyptian Vulture pair lost their nest to that fire. And then there was the local tree planting NGO who lost seven years of reforestation work. The recent spate of fires was particularly relentless, with the military called in to help try and control them. Some areas had needed evacuating, and some homes lost. Fortunately, the fire did not reach the South Africans' house, this time.

Tourism was also taking a hit because of the fires, with the South Africans just one of many who'd had guests cancel due to the fires. One family checked out the same afternoon they checked in, saying the air quality was too poor for them to stay. The president called the fires an 'attack against Asturias', and it did feel like the tide of public opinion was starting to change. However, the Asturian 'Minister of Rural Affairs and Territorial Cohesion' said the fires were part of the indigenous cultural heritage, and an important management tool. Perhaps the fires could have once been argued as this, but with the quickly changing climate the fires were taking on a life of their own, quickly becoming out of control in a way they hadn't before.

Some of our neighbours, particularly those who farmed, told us that the fires were often started by tourists flicking cigarette butts out of their car windows, or even by firemen looking to create work for themselves. Other neighbours, those who didn't farm, knew exactly who was setting the fires. The sites were always the same. As Luke said, 'you just have to look at whose cattle are grazing there when the new grass comes through.'

A few years ago, to combat the fires, a law was enacted that made it illegal to graze cattle in any burnt areas. However, the government later repealed this law, effectively sanctioning the fires. And so, on dry days with southerly winds, a small group of repeat offenders, only a few hundred in all of Astrurias, set fires to the mountains to clear them for grazing for their livestock. Few arrests were made and even fewer convictions. The rest of us left to hide from the smoke and hope that the fire didn't swallow up our homes. Sitting and waiting, feeling completely powerless and defenceless.

Beyond the fires' direct impacts there were the indirect effects it was having on the landscape. Like the elimination of tree succession, which consequently was increasing the flood risks. Just as drier times were becoming drier, so the wetter times were becoming wetter, and without forests to absorb the increased rainfall it all gathered in the flattest lowest points. The local town being particularly prone to flooding, the response was now to install seventeen million euros worth of flood defences. Luke and I often wondered how much it would cost for them to reforest the scalped hillsides that surrounded our local town.

Asturias would probably argue that they were doing their bit for reforesting, having just announced an annual increase of three hundred hectares of eucalyptus plantation, with a goal of sixty-three thousand hectares to be planted by the end of 2031. Originally from Australia, eucalyptus started being planted in the late 1950s, promoted by the central government as it was a fast-growing tree species. Plantations needed little care, and trees could be sold after twelve to fifteen years of growth, so with farming becoming less profitable, and at a time that many were migrating to the cities, converting agricultural land into eucalyptus monocultures seemed a sensible economic investment.

However, eucalyptus trees poison the soil, making it inhospitable for local trees to grow. Additionally, they offer very little to the local wildlife, as their leaves aren't eaten by deer, cows, or other local herbivores. The one exception we witnessed was our local pair of Black Woodpeckers, the largest woodpecker in Europe, nesting in a eucalyptus tree. Luke later read that at lower altitudes, eucalyptus trees are favored nesting sites for Black Woodpeckers due to their soft wood. But aside from this, eucalyptus plantations are considered green deserts.

Furthermore, they fuel wildfires because eucalyptus trees are designed to burn and then regrow under such conditions.

Despite being the wettest region in Spain, our neighboring province, Galicia, had become a wildfire hotspot. Eucalyptus is now Galicia's most abundant tree, and between 2001 and 2015, nearly forty percent of fires in the country broke out there. As a result, Galicia, alongside Portugal, enacted a moratorium on eucalyptus plantations.

Meanwhile, Asturias is not only actively planting new eucalyptus plantations but is also planning to legalize the illegal ones. Having spent decades encouraging the proliferation of eucalyptus as a way to support the timber and pulp industry, it is evident that very powerful vested interests are controlling the government's stance on the matter.

Across the valley from Wild Finca there's a eucalyptus plantation and this autumn the machinery moved in, and the trees started to come down. We now had front row seats to watch the whole eucalyptus debacle unfold. It's perhaps been somewhat of a miracle that the plantation has not been affected by the fires. Yet.

Chapter 46

That Wolfish Way

The big dog was attempting to get into the back of our car. We were in the process of sorting our snacks for the walk, and it wanted to be involved. It was a puppy in a full grown Mastín's body. It was unaware of its own size and particularly oblivious of how sharp the nail embedded anti-wolf collar it wore was, which had already caught Luke and me a few times as we'd tried to stop the creature from climbing into the boot of our car.

We'd parked in the car park above Sotres, preparing for a walk we'd done a dozen or so times before. This time we were there off the back of a week's worth of news articles about wolf sightings in the area. And so, with our friend Ewout visiting to dig more ponds with Luke, we'd packed up the car and headed to the site where the wolves had most recently been spotted. The two Mastíns that'd approached us on our arrival, the second which remained a respectable fifty metres away throughout, albeit barking aggressively, made us feel less confident about our chances of seeing said wolves. The livestock we could only assume they were guarding, were a hundred metres up the opposite mountainside.

A hunk of bread cast off to the side as a distraction kept the dog away for long enough for us to get ourselves mostly together (we don't as a rule feed the dogs, it is explicitly stated throughout the Picos de Europe that you mustn't, but in this case the scars it was causing us left us with little choice). I say mostly together, Roan wanted to stay with the dog and Luke still had something or other left to sort, so before the dog returned to try and steal more snacks, with Albus safely strapped to my back, I'd grabbed a now inconsolable Roan and struck off up the road that was our intended hike route.

We'd got quite a way before Luke caught up with us. 'Did you hear that?' We had not heard anything beyond Roan's wailing, which hadn't ceased since dragging him away from his new best friend. 'I am sure it was howling wolves,' Luke continued. I pointed out the obvious, 'are you sure it wasn't just Roan?' who did sound uncannily like a wolf. We stopped at this point and were watching a forest guard park up at the only lay-by down the valley, the same direction from where we'd just driven. Two rangers climbed out and Luke was watching them through his binoculars. 'No,' he said, 'the howls had come from the direction those rangers are now walking.'

There were a few wolf scats along the way, some relatively fresh. A couple of Chamois scampering on the rocky mountainside above us. But no wolf. With two little humans with us this wasn't entirely surprising, and so we returned to the car with every intention of packing up and heading home as quickly as possible. But our friend Ewout, who now worked at an Observatory in Belgium, had Roan enchanted by the night sky. The pair sat by the car naming every planet and moon and star until it became too cold. Only then did we set off, and just as we got to the road where the rangers had parked up, something ran across the road in front of us. Fortunately, I was taking the drive slowly and was able to quickly pull the car off right, putting my headlights on full as I stopped. Sure enough, twenty metres or so ahead of us, was a young wolf. It stood for a second and then sauntered, in that wolfish way, out of the beam of the headlights, up the hill and away from us. Luke jumped out of the car with his thermal camera and began to make a squeaking noise. It's a trick of his that calls in all manner of predators. Foxes, owls, and even a Pine Marten once, as it sounds like a dying rodent. And sure enough, the wolf stopped in its tracks, ears pricked and then it doubled back. By this point I'd turned off the car lights, and Luke had managed to hook up the thermal camera to his phone, so the rest of us were watching the wolf via this. The wolf soon lost interest in the origin of the squeaking and reverted to its route up the mountain. We were all elated with the encounter. Roan's (and Ewout's) first wolf! Poor Albus in his car seat, facing the wrong direction, had missed it all.

We are yet to have wolf or bear visit Wild Finca, but as they are one of the reasons we came to Asturias in the first place, and as they both are expected to arrive in the coming years, their anticipated return dictates a lot of our decisions. The research suggests that the bears will be arriving over the Sueve mountains in the next ten years, and so we continue to plant fruit and nut trees with the dream that one day we will wake to see a bear feasting on them. As for the wolf, many say that within the next five years they will be here more permanently, especially as at the end of September, 2021, wolf hunting was banned across the whole of Spain, to fall in-line with the EU directives. Galicia, Asturias, Cantabria and Castilla y Leon, where 95% of the wolves live, unsurprisingly protested and are in the process of appealing the decision through the courts. Irrelevant of the politics Luke and I know that when the wolf hopefully does arrive, our sheep will need to be brought in at night, maybe even some guardian dogs added to the flock.

Part 3

Growing with the Land

Chapter 47

The Loop

Come on a walk with us, a walk I've probably done a hundred times now. It starts right from our front doorstep at Wild Finca and takes us up the driveway — a bit of a hill to get the heart rate going. I've left Luke behind, layering seaweed collected from the beach yesterday onto the asparagus beds. The plums in the food forest are bursting into white blossom, and two Grasshopper Warblers are reeling somewhere on the farm.

Sometimes it's hard to pinpoint their location since they rarely take to the wing, preferring to scurry through the dense vegetation. Their song has a ventriloquial effect, and the curious way sound echoes here doesn't help with locating them. The mechanical, insect-like calls of this old-world warbler began a week ago, signaling the arrival of spring.

A few days ago, the first Egyptian Vulture passed through. Short-toed Eagles have been hunting in the fields, and a pair of Black Kites have been displaying over the orchard above us. Perez's Frogs have taken over the ponds, and their strident songs can be heard throughout the day. As each migrant returns, so a ritual of welcoming them home begins.

At the top of the driveway, we stop at the Fuente, so that I can catch my breath and to see if I can spot any newts. But today it is covered in algae and leaves.

My companions always change on this walk, today it is just Albus and me. He has been teething and miserable, but as soon as you get him outside, he calms. Roan is at school, but he and I used to do this walk, almost daily, during my maternity leave with him. It is about 4km or so, I have used it intermittently when attempting Couch to 5k. On the odd occasion I let the dogs drag me around it. More usually we ride the horses around it. We call it the Loop.

There is dew on the grass and the sound of cow bells serenades us. As we approach the road corner the Picos emerge, bathed in an ethereal mist, and nestled below is our local town. The beauty of our location is that we feel remote and wild, but we are within a five-minute drive of this vibrant little town.

Bright yellow scatters the verge, the Field Mustard is now in bloom. Yellow seems to be the colour of the day with Dandelions sprinkling the pastures where the cows graze, and I make a note to collect some when I get home for they are particularly delicious battered. And did you know that pretty much every part of the Dandelion is edible? Not just the flowers, but the leaves are like rocket, and the roots can be used for tea. In fact, that evil little weed that threatens the perfect lawn is full of antioxidants, can help to manage high blood pressure and has been shown to lower cholesterol. Not to mention what they do for the bees. When Roan was just starting to talk, he would identify them to us with a roar. Soon the Dandelion in its cottony seed formation will start to appear. One of Roan's favourite things to do is to hit them over people's heads. Blowing still a little bit tricky, and comes with a lot of spit, so he finds a good whack a more convenient seed dispersal method.

The road begins to descend as I start to pass through our little village. I spy the furrowed narrow leaves of the White Asphodel. Albus's namesake. The first has recently flowered on the rocky island at Wild Finca.

The wildflowers make my walk slow-going for there are many that I wish to stop and identify. I am no expert, and my trusty plant ID app is close to hand. I don't trust my app completely mind you, I consider it more of a starting point. Roan, who also loves the process of taking the photos and getting an ID, decided to take a photograph of Bumba the other day. The app came back with an ID of fungi. Indie and Otis both came out as Lady Orchids.

A few days ago, we were walking around Wild Finca, and with the Short-toed Eagles' return we had gone to check out the reptile mats. If the predator is around, then so should the prey be. Throughout the winter the black mat had been the home of a hibernating Garden Dormouse, only her fluffy nest remained. She had been replaced by a Smooth Snake and several Slow Worms. Roan was desperate to get hands-on with a Slow Worm. It was not his first time, and he has been incredibly lucky to have many creatures in his hand and so Luke had given him one to hold. He took it gently and inspected it, a face full of awe, and we captured the moment and shared the image on social media. The comments are always in the same vein, 'it amazes me how close to nature your little one is!' 'This little guy is so brave; he isn't afraid of anything!' I always find myself replying in a jokey manner, 'he has to be! Living here, with us.' But I think next time I need to offer a better answer, because if all children were given the same opportunity, their interest encouraged, nurtured, then I believe all children would be as enamoured and in awe of the natural world.

We pass the little village cemetery, and the plum tree that frames it is bowed over with white blossom. Down through the main strip of the village, dogs run out from all the houses to bark as we pass. One dog gets a little closer than I would like. Normally I walk with a walking stick but today I have forgotten it. It's a sensible addition to any excursion, for everyone keeps dogs in the villages, and in the mountains there are the livestock guardian dogs. I stand my ground and the dog backs off.

The hill starts to descend and at the crossroads we take a right. The sound of cow bells is exchanged for the sound of donkey bells, and a small herd look up at us as we walk by. Work is going on at the quarry. A Robin, Sardinian Warbler and Blackcap harmonise with the sound of a lorry reversing.

Sometimes at Wild Finca we hear the explosions from the quarry, when the wind is just so. But fortunately, as it is the other side of the hill to us, we don't hear much more than that.

A large purple-pink plant has erupted on the grassy roadside verge. It is the Giant Orchid. We first spotted it last spring and have been keeping an eye out for it the past few months. It's an impressive specimen, almost a metre high. Everything about it is giant. Giant leaves clasp a giant stem, and the giant flowers are arranged in a dense spike. We haven't seen one at Wild Finca yet, maybe this year.

Butterflies and bees tinker along the road verge, there are thrushes, Blackbirds and Robins galore. The new fine feather-looking Wild Fennel fronds are starting to emerge at the base of the old, dried stems, Roan's favourite snack at this time of year. Chopping the liquorice smelling fronds and putting them through an omelette is another yummy way of eating them, and a good way to use up the glut of eggs we are currently receiving.

The gorse is a close second favourite snack provider for when we are out and about. The yellow flowers taste a bit like coconut, and as it flowers all year round there are usually always some to be found. We once tried to make gorse flower syrup, but the effort was not worth the result. Far too many flowers were needed and it's nearly impossible to pick a flower without getting a little spiked, so picking lots ended up being quite painful. Plus, they are much tastier fresh.

At the bottom of the back hill, I have a choice to make. There is a cut through beneath a small copse, or I can stick to the road and walk through another village via the fig tree. The fig tree is now bare but in autumn it was always the route of choice when we are out riding the Loop. I choose the cut through today.

There is a bird circling overhead, but it is too far to identify having left my binoculars at home. So long as I remember Albus and a hat for him (which miraculously has stayed on this far, normally it's whipped off at regular intervals), there will inevitably be something I forget for myself. No matter, an opportunity to enjoy the closer moments. Like a male Blackcap alighting from the bramble vine and landing on a leafless tree branch a little further ahead of us on the path.

I may have remembered the hat, but I have forgotten the suncream, so sticking to the shady spots is the route for today. The pathway gets a little rocky, and as I start to climb, a heavy head lays against my back. Albus has spent the most part of the walk straining to look around me, but we are now approaching nap time, and the warmth has got the better of him.

The pathway gains a drystone wall on one side, covered in moss and Ivy, it is the perfect nesting spot. I keep my eyes peeled, as although it still feels a little bit early, I've been watching the birds around Wild Finca gathering nesting materials. Plus, new research has found that birds are now laying their eggs nearly a month earlier due to climate change.

I stop for a moment to pin Albus up. His hat has slipped off and his head is lolling in sleep. We have just exited the small tree tunnel, and Greater Stitchwort, Spotted Dead Nettle and Dog Violets, purple and white make up the composition of the banks now. At the end of the row, a clump of bright yellow Beaked Hawk's-beard stands in a crowd.

At the end of the summer, for an accumulation of reasons my mental health took a bit of a nosedive, and so I had looked into therapy. It would have to be something online; there aren't many English speaking anything in these parts, so I didn't fancy my chances of finding an English-speaking therapist. I sent a few emails, but whilst awaiting replies (which in the end never came), I stumbled across a foraging edible and medicinal plants course with Permacrafters, an online sustainability school. The course promised to make me an independent forager who could confidently nourish herself with dozens of wild plants. The course covered the rules of foraging safely and ethically, taught the basics of botany and chemistry. It also taught how to identify common wild plants, how to make recipes with them and how to harvest medicinal plants and prepare remedies with them. It turned out to be the therapy I needed.

I have reached the village, and the peace is shattered by a strimmer. Luke calls this sound the national anthem of Asturias. Fortunately, a cluster of bright glossy yellow star-shaped flowers distract me from the ear sore. The sun's face reflected in miniature; they are Lesser Celandines. Same family as the buttercup. I imagine they can probably tell if you like butter too, with those shiny yellow petals.

I am starting to find such a simple joy in the moment when I don't need to turn to my app for identifying, when the name rolls off my tongue unprompted. Naming the nature that I see makes me feel more connected to the land.

We pass the house with the bowed over pomelo tree, I haven't quite worked up the courage to pick one yet. We hurry by their very barky dogs, and now we are on the back pathway, the one that on the other side of the hill transects Wild Finca.

In autumn the field to my right is covered in Parasol Mushrooms which we sneak in and pick and fry up with onions and a little Lea & Perrins.

The second challenge for an unfit mummy with a sleeping sack of potatoes on her back, is the ascent of the back hill. Spots are covered with shade, but longer stretches are quite exposed and now particularly warm this spring morning. The light glimmering through the leaves, and my movement, makes it feel like I am walking under a giant crystal chandelier. Where the canopy closes, I spot the magnificent upward facing star-shaped blue blossoms of an Alpine Squill. Roan had pointed out one in our woods just a few days ago, and together we'd used the app to identify it. Now I consider the Alpine Squill a new friend, although one to be kept at arm's length, for the entire plant is poisonous and can be fatal if ingested. Fortunately, Roan touched it with a stick on our first meeting, but we washed our hands thoroughly when we got back to the house.

I look to my left, in case the deer we disturbed on our walk through the woods a few weeks back have returned. At that time, we'd been with friends; four adults, two three-year olds and two one-year olds, on a raucous romp in search of Wild Garlic and Cuckoo Flowers, and we'd disturbed the deer who'd crashed through the woods to escape. But there is no sign of them today.

At the top of the hill the valley opens up and if my breath had not already been taken by the hill, it is always taken by this view. This is my favourite part of the Loop, with the Picos, in all their glory, dead ahead and the anticipation of seeing our little finca just around the corner. Plus, by this point I've done all the hills.

The land drops steeply to my left in a tumble of gorse. I wonder if I will see a Cleopatra butterfly. They are large butterflies, the male is particularly striking, a darker yellow but with a suffusion of orange on the upper surface. When they land, the raised veins on the undersides of their wings give them the appearance of a leaf. The first time I saw one was walking the Loop in reverse, with Roan, at perhaps around the same age as Albus is now.

The stream in the valley below is boisterous today, its bubbling reverberating all the way back up to me. There is a buzzard calling and I spot the bird below. A second comes in to join it, perhaps they are courting.

The land they kettle above is where our wolf scientist told us the wolf passes. We have never seen one or had them pass any of our camera traps. But we are ready for when they do arrive. The fox has taught us many lessons. The sheep now come in at night and if the horses need to as well, then the barns are ready for them. I don't anticipate the wolf anytime soon though.

The decapitated heads of two wolves were left on the steps of the town hall in Ponga only a few days ago. After those first demonstrations when we'd first arrived, the strung-up wolf on the road sign, the bodies in the supermarket carpark, the head in the local pool, we had gone nearly three years with no more actions like it. But after the law had been passed, and the anger it had triggered, it had always felt more a question of when.

I heard an old Native American proverb recently, that the wolf was put on earth to manage the spread of man, and man to manage the spread of the wolf. In that war my money's on man. But it will be man's undoing.

The heat is starting to ramp up, so I interrupt my idle observations for it is time to get this baby home. I start to stride out, disturbing a couple of small white butterflies as I round the corner, and there is Wild Finca. The backdrop is the Picos De Europa, and disappointingly, a rather large fire on the horizon. But, on this walk, right now, I am not going to let the fires work me into my usual fury. Instead, I will focus on the butterflies. We've had Large Tortoiseshells and Large Whites so far on our walk, and there are more flitting the pathway ahead of me. One hundred and fifty-four species of butterfly have been recorded in this area, but we are yet to start a count for Wild Finca. Before we do, I will have to get better at identifying butterflies. It is on my to-do list.

The land is looking verdant green with patches of blue Birdseye Speedwell, yellow Field Mustard and Red Clover, despite the dry winter. It is in stark contrast to the neighbours' yellow, brittle, overgrazed fields, where the cows are on dirt and haylage already. A bad omen for the summer ahead which is predicted to be the driest on record.

The sound of bickering Black Woodpeckers rises from the woodland below. The calls emanate from just below the cave on our land, where we have had a trap camera set up since the turn of the new year. It has been incredibly active, with a pair of foxes denning there. Hopefully they will reveal their cubs in the next few weeks. And the coming and goings of a family of Wild Boar, the fact there has been less hunting this year evident in their regular appearances.

I have now reached the point on the pathway where on both sides of me it's Wild Finca land. It really is looking lush and colourful, and hopefully welcoming to all the migrant birds that are starting to arrive. It also feels cooler here. Most of the ponds are thriving, but I have spotted Luke at the one which keeps getting holes from a nighttime visitor. Seaweed spreading complete, he is now stood over the empty pond scratching his head. Clearly there is another leak that has become his top priority. I will have to remind him of the more pressing items on the to-do list when I get back.

And he should take the wins, for the rest of his ponds are really starting to establish themselves. Hopefully these new sources of water will attract birds that we haven't necessarily seen, or just had passing. The Nightingale perhaps. The higgledy-piggledy drystone walls, that we have attempted to restore in parts, will hopefully look homely to prospecting birds. The spiky pillows of bramble and gorse, that Luke's been cultivating, will hopefully act as another welcoming sight for other nesting birds.

A big sigh from Albus, this has clearly been a very tiring walk for him. A buzzard is perched in a leafless tree in the field to my right, on the boundary where Wild Finca meets the common land. Too busy staring at him I stumble and trip, and my sudden movement causes him to alight. These days a buzzard at a distance really could be anything, until he's not. But I'm never disappointed. They are the most underrated of raptors in my opinion. Such variety in their plumage, and behaviour. We have a regular buzzard in this particular field who will hover all afternoon if the other birds don't harass him. I often watch him with the boys from our living room window.

In the field to my left are the sheep. Most of the sensible sheep are under a tree but not Blanca, she is grazing right out in the blazing sunshine. They don't know that their fate here at Wild Finca lies in the balance. This morning, after Luke had dropped Roan at school, he returned to make a proposal to me and Albus. He wants to move the sheep on. They've been driving him nuts, eating the newly planted trees, spending all day by the ponds and damaging their banks. We've found that we can't replicate the way Rebecca manages her farm, for numerous reasons. We've also realised that we have a good population of deer, and now, due to reduced hunting pressure, boar too (although who knows if that will last). So, we don't need the sheep's grazing habits like we used to. Plus, we have the three horses, who are much easier to fence and move each day. And now Luke believes we are losing biodiversity due to the sheep. It's been a particularly dry winter, who knows what our summer will be like. The points against the sheep stack up.

Below the sheep is the first pond, by the chicken coop, and it is looking beautiful. The Mallard pair were there again this morning. It's their third spring hanging around, but in past years they have always disappeared when we go in there to feed the chickens. This year they stayed, so I have my fingers crossed that they will nest.

I've reached the back pathway to our house. The gate is open, and I get caught in a giant spider's web while closing it. I could cut through but I'm enjoying the walk, so I continue up the final incline, the last challenge this walk has for me. Here there are gaps in the tree line where you can see the heart of Wild Finca, where we live. It's a bit of a mess, if I'm completely honest. We took it on knowing it was a big job, a ten-year job at the very least. We have lived here for four years now, plans for renovating the farmhouse have been in for over a year and a half, with no news of them being signed off. The roof won't hold much longer, the cracks down the walls gaping wider after each storm. However, the scene is brightened up by the stunning mural the two American Workaways did for us on the garage door, and from here you can see it in all its glory.

A Jay shouts from up ahead, just beyond the Fuente. I wonder what has made him so angry on this beautiful day. We round the corner of our ancient apple tree and start back down the hill to home. The Swallow pair are feeding on the wing overhead. They had us worried for a bit, the male arrived two weeks earlier than its mate and would sit lonely on the power line that hangs across the driveway. Last year they fledged two broods from the old grain barn. What could have happened to her? She finally appeared one afternoon, while I'd been hanging out the washing, and their chattering had been euphoric. She'd then come and sat on the wire closest to me and continued her chirruping, catching me up on her gruelling journey back from spending the winter in South Africa.

Overjoyed, I'd gone to tell Luke of her return and the pair's reunion. 'Got caught in a sandstorm over the Sahara, absolute nightmare, nearly didn't think I'd make it back here! Anyway, better getting cracking if we are to match last year's numbers!' Luke said, in his best Swallow impression. And sure enough, we'd caught them in the act the very next day. Unfortunately, they have lost last year's nest site in the old silo, for a Wren has commandeered it. Hopefully they take to the downstairs of the new walnut loft, the window of which we've left open specially.

I reach the driveway and walk into the vegetable patch. Bumblebees, as big as wine gums, are busy tending to the flowers. They flit between the Spotted Dead-nettles and a few early-flowering Borage that have gone wild across the veggie patch, their nectars of choice. We have a family afternoon of seed planting ahead of us. We will sow a few now and then again in a few weeks in case the seeds fail, or something eats them, but also so that our plants don't all come good in one go. Yellow, orange and red carrots, and multi-coloured beetroots are on the to-do list for today. I overheard Roan on the phone to my parents the other day, being shown around their sole raised bed. Grandpa was listing what he had in there, some herbs, tomatoes, broccoli, a few lettuces. Do you have carrots, Roan asked. No, answered Grandpa. Do you have strawberries, Roan asked. No, answered Grandpa. Well, you had better go and get some then hadn't you, he said, quite matter of fact.

I can see Luke walking toward us from the pond, Albus is waking, and soon it will be time to collect Roan from school. As I observe these moments, a question that recently resonated with me comes to mind: What sort of ancestor do I want to be? This question has begun to occupy my thoughts, guiding and shaping my daily choices as I reflect on the legacy I wish to leave behind.

I want to be remembered for the wild spaces I leave behind. The future of Wild Finca will always prioritize our wild neighbours, with every decision rooted in respect and with the best of intentions.

I want to be remembered as someone who inspired people to seek a deeper connection to nature. As Roan and Albus grow, their fascination and passion for the natural world inspire an even greater calling to share the magic of Wild Finca and invite others to experience her.

And I want to be remembered as hopeful. Hope can be such powerful catalyst for change. Perhaps we can all live with a bit more hope—not the kind made of dreams, but the kind made of action. By embracing hope and living with intention, I truly believe that one day soon we can all enjoy a paradise with wolves.

From the Author

Thank you for gifting your time to my book, *No Paradise with Wolves*. If you have a moment, I would be incredibly grateful if you could write a review on your favorite online site.

If you're curious about what we're up to at Wild Finca and want to stay connected, please visit our website and sign up for the Wild Finca newsletter at www.wildfinca.com.

With greatest thanks,
Katie Stacey

ENVIRONMENT

Earth Books are practical, scientific and philosophical publications about our relationship with the environment. Earth Books explore sustainable ways of living; including green parenting, gardening, cooking and natural building. They also look at ecology, conservation and aspects of environmental science, including green energy. An understanding of the interdependence of all living things is central to Earth Books, and therefore consideration of our relationship with other animals is important. Animal welfare is explored. The purpose of Earth Books is to deepen our understanding of the environment and our role within it. The books featured under this imprint will both present thought-provoking questions and offer practical solutions. If you have enjoyed this book, why not tell other readers by posting a review on your preferred book site.

Safe Planet

Renewable Energy Plus Workers' Power
John Cowsill
Safe Planet lays out a roadmap of renewable energy sources
and meteorological data to direct us towards a safe planet
. Paperback: 978-1-78099-682-0 ebook: 978-1-78099-683-7

Approaching Chaos

Could an Ancient Archetype Save 21st Century Civilization?
Lucy Wyatt
Civilisation can survive by learning from the social, spiritual
and technological secrets of ancient civilisations such as Egypt.
Paperback: 978-1-84694-255-6

Gardening with the Moon & Stars

Elen Sentier
Organics with Ooomph! Bringing biodynamics to the ordinary
gardener.
Paperback: 978-1-78279-984-9 ebook: 978-1-78279-985-6

GreenSpirit

Path to a New Consciousness
Marian Van Eyk McCain
A collection of essays on 21st Century green spirituality and its
key role in creating a peaceful and sustainable world.
Paperback: 978-1-84694-290-7 ebook: 978-1-78099-186-3

The Protein Myth

Significantly Reducing the Risk of Cancer, Heart Disease,
Stroke, and Diabetes While Saving the Animals and the Planet
David Gerow Irving
The Protein Myth powerfully illustrates how the way to vibrant
health and a peaceful world is to stop exploiting animals.
Paperback: 978-1-84694-673-8 ebook: 978-1-78099-073-6

This Is Hope
Green Vegans and the New Human Ecology How We Find Our
Way to a Humane and Environmentally Sane Future
Will Anderson
This Is Hope compares the outcomes of two human ecologies;
one is tragic, the other full of promise...
Paperback: 978-1-78099-890-9

Readers of ebooks can buy or view any of these bestsellers by
clicking on the live link in the title. Most titles are published
in paperback and as an ebook. Paperbacks are available in
traditional bookshops. Both print and ebook formats are
available online.

Find more titles and sign up to our readers' newsletter
www.collectiveinkbooks.com